Refrigerant Charging and Service Procedures for Air Conditioning:
Workbook
Preamble

The <u>author</u>, Craig Migliaccio, is a licensed Career and Technical Education Teacher of HVACR (Heating, Ventilating, Air Conditioning, and Refrigeration), Sheet Metal, and Building Maintenance, in the State of New Jersey in the United States of America. Craig is also the owner of an HVACR contracting business with over 17 years of experience in the field. Communication with technicians across the United States, Canada, and other countries led Craig to develop the "Refrigerant Charging and Service Procedures for Air Conditioning" book and workbook as resources for those who want to grow in the understanding of air conditioning and refrigeration systems. The goal is to provide comprehensive study material that includes information on refrigerants and the refrigeration cycle all the way through to the charging and troubleshooting of these refrigerant based systems. Videos of procedures may be found at www.youtube.com/acservicetechchannel and at www.acservicetech.com.

<u>Contributors:</u> Frank Ackley (Question Development)
Brandon Price (Layout and Design)

<u>Illustrators:</u> Brandon Price (Images, Layout and Design, Cover)
Olivia VanDeventer (Images)
Micah Wenker (Images)

<u>References:</u> EPA, Environmental Protection Agency, 27 Feb. 2019, www.epa.gov/
Migliaccio, Craig. *Refrigerant Charging and Service Procedures
for Air Conditioning.* AC Service Tech LLC, 29 May 2019

ISBN# 978-1-7338172-2-6

Disclaimer

The author, Craig Migliaccio, AC Service Tech LLC, and any other entities involved with the creation of this workbook, under no circumstances, shall be held responsible for any damage or physical harm to persons or property or losses of any nature that may occur as a result of any interpretation and/or application of information, procedures, testing, or descriptions stated in this workbook and answer key.

Although the author, Craig Migliaccio, and AC Service Tech LLC have made every effort to ensure that information in this workbook is correct and current at the date of publication, the author, Craig Migliaccio, and AC Service Tech LLC do not assume and hereby disclaim any liability to any party for any loss, damage, or disruption caused by errors and/or omissions, whether such errors and/or omissions result from negligence, accident, or any other cause. Any and all manufacturer installation and service literature and code books, along with their recommended practices, shall supersede any recommendations or procedures mentioned in the "Refrigerant Charging and Service Procedures for Air Conditioning" book, workbook, and answer key.

This workbook is not designed or intended to act as a stand alone instructional reference, but rather is meant to be a compliment to the "Refrigerant Charging and Service Procedures for Air Conditioning" book. All information within is based and/or derived from information available within the aforementioned text.

Always wear safety glasses, butyl lined gloves, and other PPE (Personal Protective Equipment) prior to accessing a system's refrigerant charge. Always make sure to have fresh air available or wear a SCBA (Self-Contained Breathing Apparatus) and never breathe in refrigerant gases. For more information on safety, refer to the refrigerant specific SDS (Safety Data Sheet, formally known as Material Safety Data Sheet) for each refrigerant prior to handling. Make sure to follow all other safety rules stated through https://www.epa.gov and https://www.epa.gov/section608 as well as through an approved EPA 608 certification testing agency. In the United States of America, technicians must have the appropriate EPA 608 Type 1, Type 2, Type 3, or Universal Certification prior to working on any refrigerant based system or buying refrigerant. Be sure to follow all local laws, codes, and requirements.

CHAPTER 1

Understanding Refrigerants and the Refrigeration Cycle

Fill in the blanks with the correct word(s).

1. The _____ is the fluid used to transfer heat from one part of the

   refrigeration system to the other part.

2. Refrigerants vary from each other in environmental friendliness, availability, cost,

   _____ and _____.

3. Identify the chemical elements in the three following refrigerant types: CFC, HCFC, and HFC.

   a. CFC: _____ , _____ , _____

   b. HCFC: _____ , _____ , _____ , _____

   c. HFC: _____ , _____ , _____

4. Match the type of refrigerant (<u>CFC</u>, <u>HCFC</u>, <u>HFC</u>) with the correct refrigerant bottle below.

   R-410A   R-22   R-12

   a. _____   b. _____   c. _____

5. R-22 may be found in automobiles, air conditioning units, and in _____ units.

6. List the chemical compound for each of the following refrigerant types.

   a. HFO: _____

   b. HC: _____

7. All HC refrigerants are highly _____.

8. An example of an HC refrigerant is _____.

9. Individuals who violate EPA Section 608 regulations may be fined $_____ or more per

   day and per occurrence.

10. What do these abbreviations stand for?

    a. ODP: _____ _____ _____

    b. GWP: _____ _____ _____

1

Match the left hand column items with those in the right hand column.

11. _____ Global Warming Potential...   a. are highly flammable.

12. _____ Natural refrigerants...   b. is caused by the release of chlorine based refrigerants.

13. _____ Ozone depletion...   c. is a nonflammable natural refrigerant.

14. _____ HC refrigerants...   d. have no chlorine and no fluorine.

15. _____ Carbon dioxide...   e. is based on the amount of greenhouse gases.

Circle the best answer for each statement/question.

16. Which of the following types of refrigerant have ODP? **Circle all that apply.**

    a. CFC   b. HCFC   c. HFC   d. HC

17. Which of the following have GWP? **Circle the best answer.**

    a. CFC   b. HCFC   c. HFC   d. All of the above

18. Which of the following is **NOT** a CFC, HCFC, or HFC?

    a. R-290   b. R-410A   c. R-22   d. R-12

19. R-410A refrigerant is commonly used in which of the following?

    a. Air conditioning units   b. Refrigerators

    c. Commercial refrigeration units   d. All of the above

20. Which of these was the first widely used refrigerant?

    a. CFC   b. HCFC   c. HFC   d. HFO

21. Which natural refrigerant is nonflammable but has a limited scope of use due to its triple point and critical point?

    a. R-410A   b. Hydrogen   c. Carbon Dioxide   d. Propane

Circle T for True or F for False.

22. **T / F** CFC's have a low ODP.

23. **T / F** Natural refrigerants have no ODP but high GWP.

24. **T / F** Carbon dioxide is a Natural Refrigerant.

25. **T / F** The release of chlorine based refrigerants into the atmosphere is a major cause of ozone depletion.

26. **T / F** HFC's have chlorine and therefore have ODP.

27. **T / F** In an air conditioning system, the refrigerant absorbs heat from air, occupants, and/or other objects and rejects it in an outside environment.

Circle the best answer for each statement/question.

28. Which of these best describe natural refrigerants? **Circle all that apply.**

    a. Highest GWP   b. Lowest GWP   c. No ODP   d. Highest ODP

29. A packaged refrigerator or freezer with less than 5 lb of refrigerant is an example of a...

    a. Type I unit.   b. Type II unit.

    c. Type III unit.   d. Type I and Type III unit.

30. An individual with this certification is allowed to service and dispose of all appliance types.

    a. Type I Certification   b. Type II Certification

    c. Type III Certification   d. Universal Certification

31. A centrifugal chiller system with 200 lb of refrigerant is an example of a...

    a. Type I unit.   b. Type II unit.

    c. Type III unit.   d. Type I and Type II unit.

32. A split system air conditioner that has 60 lb of R-410A refrigerant is an example of a...

    a. Type I unit.   b. Type II unit.

    c. Type III unit.   d. Type II and Type III unit.

33. To earn a Universal 608 Certification, a technician must pass these parts of the test.

    a. Core and Type I   b. Core, Type I, Type II and Type III

    c. Type I and Type II   d. Type I, Type II and Type III

34. Which of the following may happen to individuals in the United States, who violate EPA Section 608 regulations?

    a. Loss of their Section 608 Certification   b. Assigned time in jail

    c. Be fined   d. All of the above

Fill in the blanks with the correct word(s).

35. In a refrigerator, the refrigerant _____ the heat and moves it outside to _____ it.

36. Refrigerants, like water, have multiple states such as solid, _____, and _____.

37. In the United States of America, the_____ regulates who can buy and work with refrigerants.

38. What does BTU stand for? _____ _____ _____

39. Define what a BTU is. _____

_____

Match the left hand column items with those in the right hand column.

Match the type of certification with the appliance that may be serviced or disposed.

40. _____ Type I Certification   a. Appliances that are low pressure

41. _____ Type II Certification   b. Appliances that are medium, high or very high pressure

42. _____ Type III Certification   c. All appliances

43. _____ Universal Certification   d. Appliances with 5 lb or less of refrigerant that are packaged and sealed by the factory

Fill in the blanks with the correct word(s).

44. The refrigerant in a refrigerant bottle is in the _____ state when both liquid and vapor are present in the bottle at the same time.

45. If the temperature surrounding a refrigerant bottle lowers, the pressure inside the bottle _____.

46. If the temperature surrounding a refrigerant bottle increases, the refrigerant inside absorbs heat, resulting in an increase of _____ inside the bottle.

47. The refrigerant inside an air conditioner is in the _____ state while the unit is off and the pressures are equalized.

48. While an air conditioning system is running, the saturated state can only be found in the _____ and the _____.

49. When the HVACR system is running, the refrigerant changes from a _____ to a _____ in the **evaporator**.

50. When the HVACR system is running, the refrigerant changes from a _____ to a _____ in the **condenser**.

51. The refrigeration cycle can be accomplished with a pressure increase at the _____ and a pressure reduction at the _____.

CHAPTER 2
The Refrigeration Cycle,
Components, Definitions, and Locations

1. Fill in the blanks in the refrigeration cycle diagram.

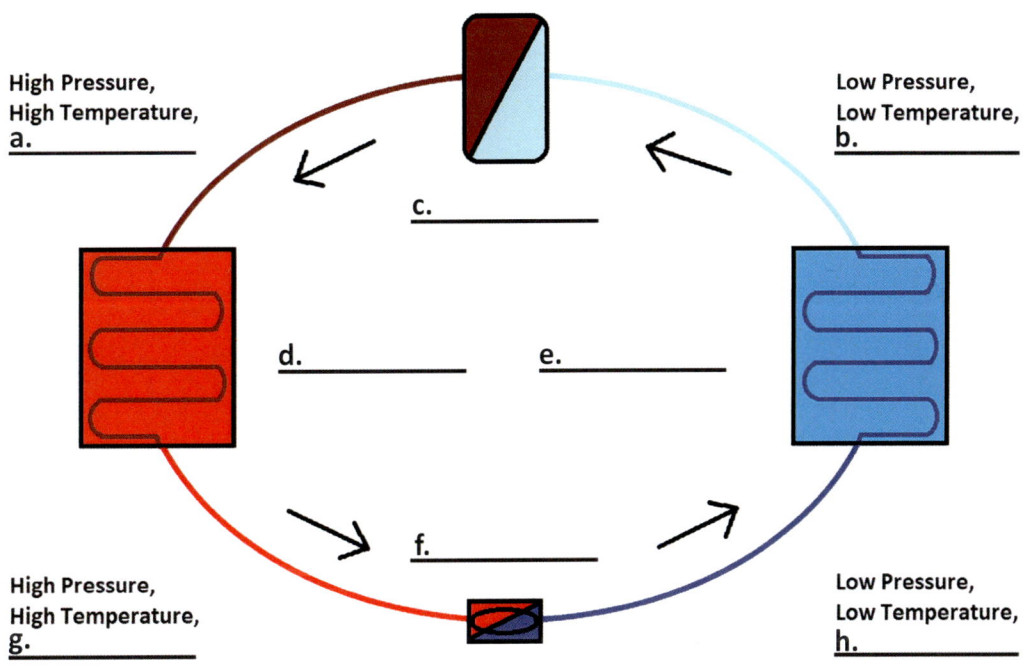

High Pressure,
High Temperature,
a._____

Low Pressure,
Low Temperature,
b._____

c._____

d._____   e._____

High Pressure,
High Temperature,
g._____

Low Pressure,
Low Temperature,
h._____

f._____

Fill in the blanks with the correct word(s).

2. The main goal of a basic refrigeration system is to _____

temperature in an area by removing _____ from it.

3. At the **compressor**, the refrigerant enters as a low pressure, low temperature superheated

_____ and exits as a high pressure, high temperature, superheated _____.

4. In the **condenser**, the refrigerant _____ heat.

5. At the **condenser**, the refrigerant enters as a high pressure, high temperature superheated vapor and

exits as a high pressure, high temperature, _____ liquid.

Circle the best answer for each statement/question.

6. At the **metering device,** the refrigerant enters as a high pressure, high temperature liquid and exits as a

low pressure, low temperature _____.

    a. liquid   b. solid   c. vapor   d. None of the above

7. At the **evaporator**, the refrigerant enters as a low pressure, low temperature liquid and exits as a low pressure, low temperature _____.

      a. superheated liquid   b. subcooled liquid

      c. superheated vapor   d. subcooled vapor

8. Superheat occurs when the refrigerant gains heat after it has changed from a saturated state into a _____ state.

      a. solid   b. vapor   c. liquid   d. All of the above

9. _____ occurs when the refrigerant loses heat after it has changed from a saturated refrigerant to a liquid.

      a. Superheating   b. Subcooling   c. Total Superheating   d. Saturation

Match the left hand column items with those in the right hand column.

10. _____ Compressor

a. Both liquid and vapor exist at the same moment, in the same location

11. _____ Evaporator coil

b. The refrigerant is in the boiled state as a gas

12. _____ Saturated

c. Where the refrigerant absorbs heat and changes to a vapor

13. _____ Service valve with port

d. Pressurizes vapor refrigerant

14. _____ Subcooling

e. The temp decrease of liquid refrigerant below its saturated temp

15. _____ Superheat

f. Allows the flow of refrigerant to be shut off for servicing and provides an access to read system pressures

16. _____ Condenser Coil

g. The temp increase of vapor refrigerant above its saturated temp

17. _____ Vapor

h. Where the refrigerant rejects heat and changes to a liquid

Circle T for True or F for False.

18. **T / F** "Change in state" is another way of saying "phase change".

19. **T / F** During the phase change, the refrigerant is in the saturated state.

20. **T / F** One phase change occurs in the evaporator.

21. **T / F** The other phase change occurs at the compressor.

22. **T / F** The two components that separate the high pressure and the low pressure sides of an air conditioning system are the metering device and the compressor.

23. **T / F** The four main components of the refrigeration cycle are the compressor, evaporator, filter drier, and metering device.

Put the correct word/term from the Word Bank next to its definition.

WORD BANK: *accumulator, filter drier, line set, metering device, receiver, reversing valve*

24. _____: Installed on the liquid line to trap any water

and debris from flowing through the system

25. _____: Comprised of a large vapor tube and a small

liquid tube

26. _____: A tank that stores subcooled liquid in a location

after the condenser but before the metering device

27. _____: A restriction that causes the refrigerant to

reduce in pressure in order to expand; can be fixed or regulating

28. _____: Changes the direction of the refrigerant flow in

a system

29. _____: A tank that protects the compressor by only

allowing vapor refrigerant to enter the suction side of the compressor

Answer the following with complete sentences.

30. How is a regulating metering device such as a TXV <u>different</u> than a piston metering device?

_____

_____

_____

31. Explain what role the compressor has in separating the high and low sides of a system.

_____

_____

_____

32. Explain what role the metering device has in separating the high and low sides of a system.

_____

_____

_____

CHAPTER 3
The Steps of the Refrigeration Cycle

1. Label the components in the image below.

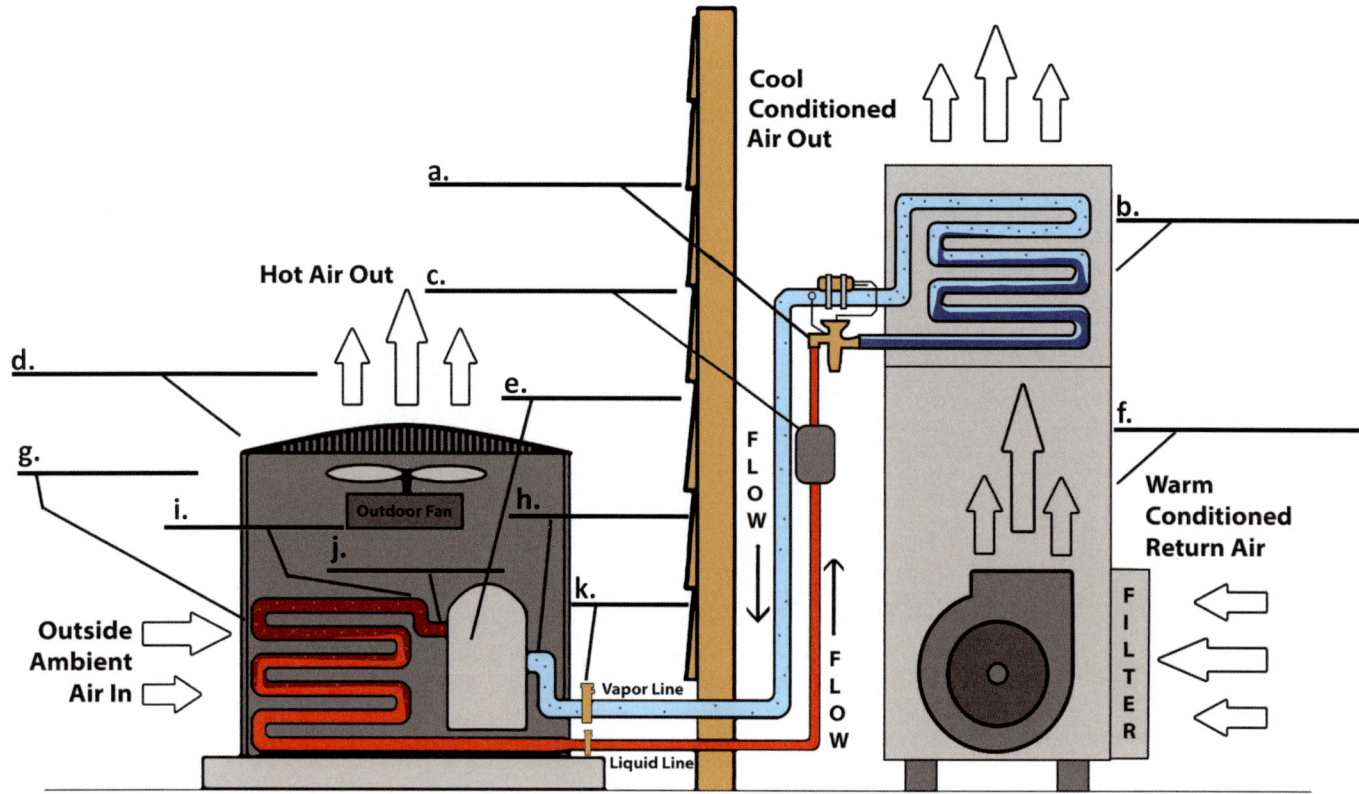

Number the following steps of the "refrigeration cycle of an air conditioner" in order from Step 1-5.

2. Step # _____: Saturated refrigerant changes to liquid in the condenser.

3. Step # _____: High temp vapor refrigerant rejects heat in the condenser (desuperheating).

4. Step # _____: Liquid refrigerant subcools in the condenser.

5. Step # _____: Vapor refrigerant enters the compressor.

6. Step # _____: High temp vapor refrigerant exits the compressor.

Number the following steps of the "refrigeration cycle of an air conditioner" in order from Step 6-10.

7. Step # _____ : Liquid refrigerant enters the metering device.

8. Step # _____ : Liquid refrigerant exits the metering device and rapidly changes to a 80% liquid, 20% vapor mix.

9. Step # _____ : Liquid refrigerant rejects heat in the condenser and lowers in temperature (subcooling).

10. Step # _____ : The refrigerant is in a fully saturated state.

11. Step # _____ : Liquid refrigerant exits the condenser and flows through the filter drier.

Number the following steps of the "refrigeration cycle of an air conditioner" in order from Step 11-15.

12. Step # _____ : Vapor refrigerant absorbs heat in the evaporator and increases in temperature until it leaves the evaporator (superheat).

13. Step # _____ : Vapor refrigerant leaves the evaporator and enters the outdoor unit vapor service port where total superheat can be measured.

14. Step # _____ : Vapor refrigerant re-enters the compressor.

15. Step # _____ : Saturated refrigerant absorbs heat in the evaporator but does not rise in temperature.

16. Step # _____ : Saturated refrigerant changes completely into a vapor.

Circle T for True or F for False.

17. **T / F** Low pressure, low temperature superheated liquid refrigerant enters the compressor.

18. **T / F** Superheated vapor exits the compressor and travels through the discharge line to the condenser.

19. **T / F** The superheated vapor rejects heat in the condenser coil and the refrigerant becomes saturated.

20. **T / F** The saturated refrigerant in the condenser rejects heat, but does not lower in temperature while in the saturated state.

21. **T / F** The saturated refrigerant in the condenser rejects heat and changes completely into a liquid.

22. **T / F** Once all the refrigerant is in the liquid state in the condenser, the refrigerant's temperature starts to rise.

23. **T / F** Saturated refrigerant absorbs heat in the evaporator and changes to a liquid.

24. **T / F** Saturated refrigerant changes into a vapor in the evaporator and then lowers in temperature.

25. **T / F** Superheated vapor refrigerant exits the evaporator.

Define the following.

26. **Subcooling:** _____

_____

27. **Superheat:** _____

_____

28. **Total Superheat:** _____

_____

_____

Fill in the blanks with the correct word(s).

29. The _____ _____ traps debris and water molecules.

30. The liquid refrigerant enters the evaporator coil as a liquid, but quickly changes to approximately 80% _____ and 20% _____ .

31. The refrigerant _____ heat in the evaporator coil.

32. A _____ _____ is an example of a bidirectional refrigerant based system that is capable of either absorbing or rejecting heat in an area.

33. The heat absorption and heat rejection areas switch depending on the directional flow of the _____ .

34. A heat pump has a _____ valve, an accumulator, and two _____ _____ .

35. The _____ is a tank that protects the compressor by preventing any unwanted saturated refrigerant from entering the compressor inlet.

Circle T for True or F for False.

36. **T / F** A TXV and a TEV are the same type of metering device.

37. **T / F** The TXV controls the subcooling in a system.

38. **T / F** Subcooling measurements are usually used to measure the superheat on an air conditioning system that has a TXV.

39. **T / F** A piston and a capillary tube are examples of TXV's.

40. **T / F** A fixed orifice can both read and adjust the superheat.

41. **T / F** The piston size can be changed by replacing the piston within the piston chamber.

42. **T / F** Total superheat is used to check and adjust the refrigerant level in an air conditioning system that has a fixed orifice metering device.

43. **T / F** A metering device is a restriction that causes the refrigerant to reduce in pressure in order to expand.

Number the following steps of the "heat pump refrigeration cycle in <u>cooling mode</u>" in order from Step 1-5.

44.	Step # _____: High pressure, high temperature, superheated vapor travels through the discharge line toward the reversing valve.

45.	Step # _____: High pressure, high temperature, superheated vapor travels through the reversing valve toward the condenser.

46.	Step # _____: High pressure, high temperature, superheated vapor enters the condenser where it de-superheats and rejects heat, lowering in temperature.

47.	Step # _____: High pressure, high temperature, superheated vapor exits the compressor.

48.	Step # _____: Low pressure, low temperature, superheated vapor refrigerant enters the vapor compressor.

Number the following steps of the "heat pump refrigeration cycle in <u>heating mode</u>" in order from Step 1-5.

49.	Step # _____: High pressure, high temperature, superheated vapor travels through the vapor service valve and heads toward the indoor condenser.

50.	Step # _____: High pressure, high temperature, superheated vapor exits the compressor.

51.	Step # _____: High pressure, high temperature, superheated vapor travels through the discharge line toward the reversing valve.

52.	Step # _____: Low pressure, low temperature, superheated vapor enters the vapor compressor.

53.	Step # _____: High pressure, high temperature, superheated vapor travels through the reversing valve and heads toward the vapor service valve.

Name the metering device type.

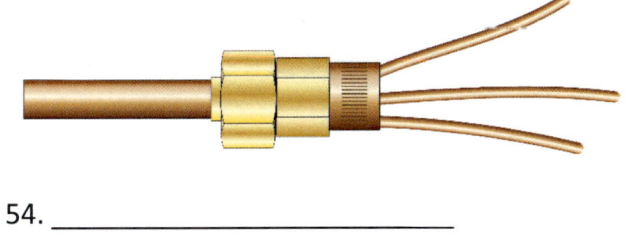

54. _____

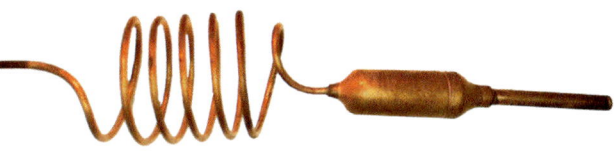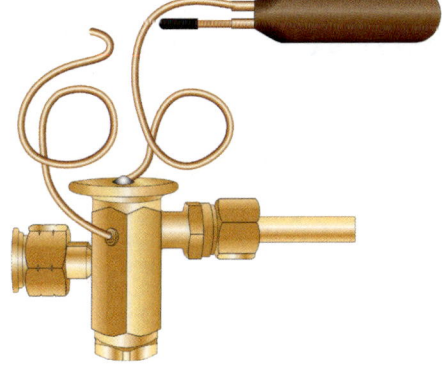

55. _____   56. _____

Solve the following.

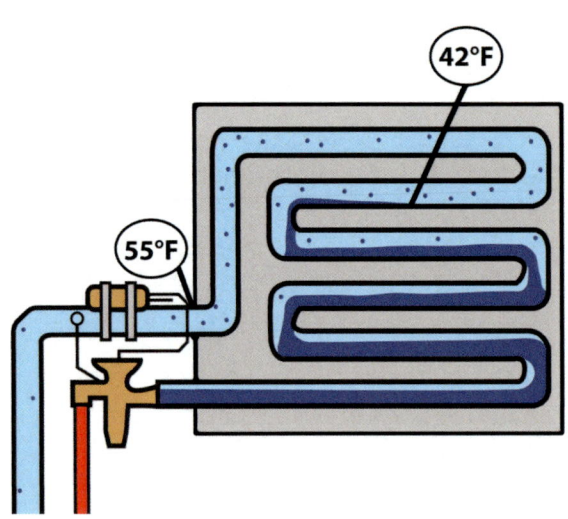

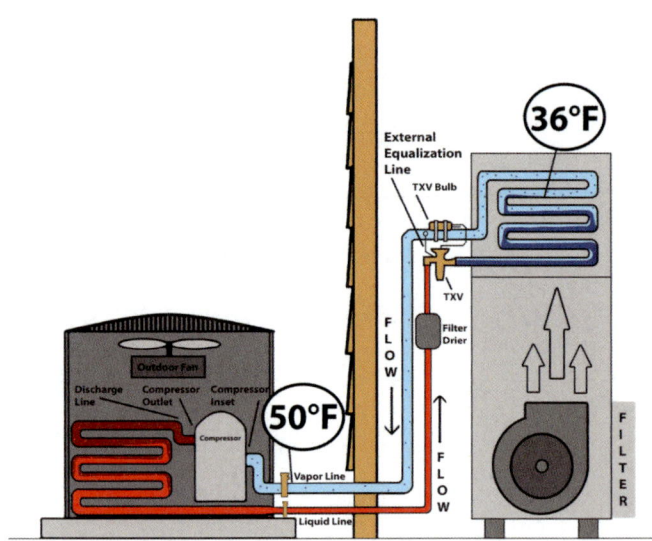

57. **Find the sat temp, actual temp on the vapor line, and the actual superheat from this image.**

a. Saturated temp: _____

b. Actual temp on the vapor line: _____

Equation: Superheat = Actual Temp – Sat Temp

c. Superheat: _____

58. **Find the sat temp, actual temp on the vapor line, and the actual total superheat from this image.**

a. Saturated temp: _____

b. Actual temp on the vapor line: _____

Equation: Total Superheat = Actual Temp – Sat Temp

c. Total Superheat: _____

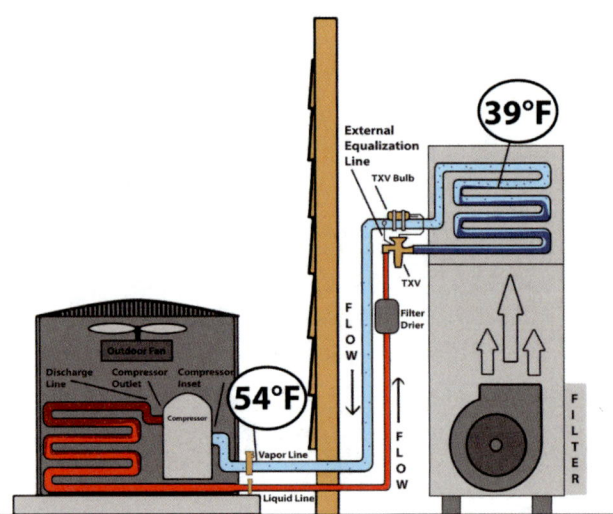

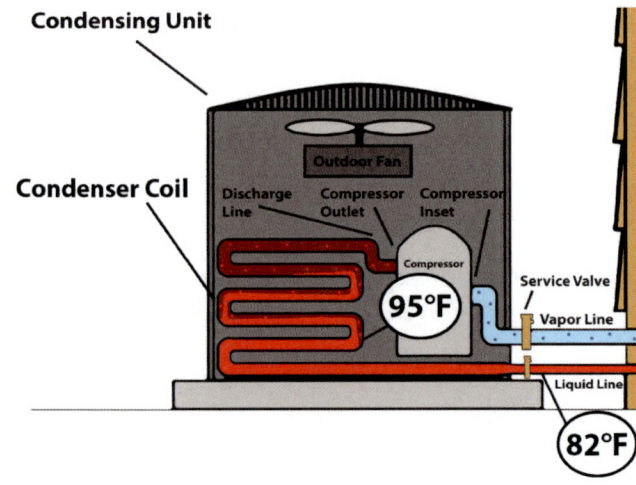

59. **Find the sat temp, actual temp on the vapor line, and the actual total superheat from this image.**

a. Saturated temp: _____

b. Actual temp on the vapor line: _____

Equation: Total Superheat = Actual Temp – Sat Temp

c. Total Superheat: _____

60. **Find the sat temp, actual temp on the liquid line, and the actual subcooling from this image.**

a. Saturated temp: _____

b. Actual temp on the liquid line: _____

Equation: Subcooling = Sat Temp – Actual Temp

c. Subcooling: _____

CHAPTER 4
Refrigerant Pressure and Temperature

Circle T for True or F for False.

1. **T / F** A P/T chart is a Pressure/Time chart.

2. **T / F** If the pressure of a saturated refrigerant is known, the temperature of the refrigerant can be determined by using a P/T chart.

3. **T / F** When the temperature is known, the pressure cannot be determined using a P/T chart.

4. **T / F** As the temperature in a refrigerant bottle lowers, the pressure inside the bottle rises.

5. **T / F** The pressure in a bottle with 1 ounce of liquid refrigerant will be the same as the pressure in a bottle with 10 lb of liquid refrigerant as long as the temperature of both bottles are the same.

Fill in the blanks with the correct word(s) to make each sentence true.

6. The refrigerant in an HVACR system is in the _____ state when the system is off and equalized.

7. _____ means that the pressure on both the low and high sides of the system are the same.

8. Most P/T charts have one guide column on the far left which either lists the

   _____ or _____.

9. PSI stands for _____ per _____ _____.

Use the P/T chart (Figure 4-8 found on page 40 of the textbook) to answer questions.

10. If the temp of an R-410A refrigerant bottle is 70° F, what is the pressure?

    a. 121 psi   b. 141 psi   c. 201 psi   d. 235 psi

11. If the temp of a refrigerant bottle is 80° F and the pressure reads 144 PSI, the refrigerant in the bottle is...

    a. R-22.   b. R-407A.   c. R-407C.   d. R-410A.

12. For each refrigerant listed on the P/T chart, if the temp increases...

    a. the pressure increases.   b. the pressure decreases.

    c. the pressure remains the same.   d. None of the above

13. What refrigerant is in the unlabeled refrigerant recovery bottle? The bottle pressure is 121 psi and has been at a constant temperature of 70° F for 4 hours. The refrigerant in the bottle is...

    a. R-410A.   b. R-22.   c. R-407A.   d. R-407C.

Circle T for True or F for False.

14. **T / F** Before using a new reusable recovery bottle, the bottle must be vacuumed.

15. **T / F** The refrigerant inside an unlabeled recovery bottle can be identified by measuring the temperature of the bottle and the pressure inside the bottle.

16. **T / F** A new refrigerant bottle that is pink or light rose colored contains R-22.

17. **T / F** A new refrigerant bottle that is light brown contains R-22.

18. **T / F** Reusable recovery bottles are always yellow and gray.

19. **T / F** If a new recovery bottle is not vacuumed prior to adding refrigerant, the P/T measurements will not correctly identify the refrigerant in the bottle.

20. **T / F** Before adding refrigerant into a recovery bottle for the first time, the bottle should be vacuumed down to a level of 4500 microns.

Fill in the blanks with the correct word(s) to make each sentence true.

21. To perform a complete vacuum procedure on a recovery bottle, the following are needed:

    a vacuum hose, a vacuum _____ and a vacuum _____.

22. After some refrigerant has been added to an empty, vacuumed recovery bottle to add pressure, the

    _____ type of refrigerant can be added to the existing charge.

23. It is very important NOT to mix _____ refrigerants in the same recovery bottle.

24. Make sure not to contaminate the refrigerant in a recovery bottle with _____,

    nitrogen, _____ vapor, or another refrigerant.

25. Instead of using a refrigerant manifold gauge set and P/T chart to determine the refrigerant in a

    system, a tool such as a refrigerant _____ can be used.

Number the following steps in order from Step 1-3 when trying to determine the refrigerant inside an air conditioning system that is off and equalized.

26.   Step # _____: Convert the pressure to the saturated temperature of possible refrigerants

                    using a P/T chart.

27.   Step # _____: Compare the actual temperature surrounding the unit to the saturated temperature

                    of multiple refrigerants to find which refrigerant is the closest match.

28.   Step # _____: Measure the pressure on the equalized system.

Circle T for True and F for False.

29. **T / F** A manifold gauge set usually comes as a single port model.

30. **T / F** The display on a manifold set may be digital or a compound gauge.
31. **T / F** The saturated temperatures of six different refrigerants can be seen on the face of most compound manifold gauges.
32. **T / F** The needle on the compound gauge points to both the pressure and the saturated temperature of the refrigerant.
33. **T / F** To measure the saturated temp of a refrigerant that is not listed on the compound gauge face, a separate P/T chart can be used to convert the pressure to saturated temperature.
34. **T / F** A manifold gauge set must be zeroed before use, especially if there is a change in elevation.

Match the beginning of each sentence with the correct ending.

35. _____ Systems that are converted from one refrigerant to another…

a. the refrigerant at the evaporator and the condenser.

36. _____ R-407C can be used as a retrofit refrigerant for R-22 as long as…

b. the middle of both the evaporator and condenser.

37. _____ Distinguishing between R-22 and an R-22 alternative (retrofit) refrigerant…

c. the system should be labeled with the new type of oil.

38. _____ If the original refrigerant oil is replaced with another type of oil,…

d. the system contains POE oil.

39. _____ When the system is running, the refrigerant is in the saturated state in…

e. is difficult using a P/T chart and reading pressure.

40. _____ If the pressures of a running system are measured, the P/T chart can be used to determine the saturated temperature of…

f. must be labeled with the new refrigerant.

Answer the following.

41. What does PSIG stand for? _____
42. What does PSIA stand for? _____
43. What is the actual surrounding air pressure at sea level? _____

Fill in the blanks with the correct word(s).

44. On the compound gauge, inches of Hg are measured from 0" Hg to _____.

45. Measurements below 0 PSIG are usually read in inches of mercury, but can also be read in

    _____.

46. In the United States of America, recovery and pump down levels of refrigerants are mandated by the

    EPA in Section _____.

47. The blue hose leading from the blue low side gauge gets connected to the large _____

    line service port during air conditioning mode.

48. The red hose leading from the red high side gauge gets connected to the small _____

    line service port during air conditioning mode.

49. The system may need to run for up to _____ minutes before an accurate saturated pressure

    can be read.

Circle the best answer for each statement/question.

50. Zero PSIG equals...

    a. 0 PSIA at sea level.   b. 100 PSIA at sea level.

    c. 14.696 PSIA at sea level.   d. None of the above

51. To determine the PSIA...

    a. add 14.696 to the PSIG.   b. subtract 14.696 from the PSIA.

    c. multiply 14.696 by the PSIG.   d. divide 14.696 by the PSIG.

52. " Hg is short for...

    a. inches of nitrogen.   b. inches of water column.

    c. inches of atmosphere.   d. inches of mercury.

53. A typical compound gauge shows measurements in...

    a. PSIG.   b. Inches of Hg.

    c. PSIG and Inches of Hg.   d. PSIG and PSIA.

54. 0 PSIG equals...

    a. 1000" Hg.   b. 100" Hg.

    c. 10" Hg.   d. 0" Hg.

Circle T for True or F for False.

55. **T / F** The yellow hose that is connected to the center of the 3 port manifold gauge set is

    called the pump down hose.

56. **T / F** Charging Refrigerant is the term used for adding refrigerant to a system.

57. **T / F** Recovery is the act of removing refrigerant from a system and storing it in a recovery bottle.

58. **T / F** When charging a system, the system always needs to be off.

59. **T / F** When charging, the refrigerant bottle can be connected to the yellow hose on the

 manifold gauge set.

Use the word bank below to answer the following questions.

blue gauge   *blue hose*   *condenser*   *evaporator*   *high side*   *large line*   *liquid*

low side   *red gauge*   *red hose*   *small line*   *suction*   *vapor*

60. Write the 7 terms from the Word Bank that are linked to measuring Total Superheat.

 _____

 _____

61. Write the remaining 6 terms from the Word Bank that are linked to measuring Subcooling.

 _____

 _____

Circle the best answer for each statement/question.

62. When is it best to purge the air out of the hoses when charging a system?

   a. when charging is finished   b. during the charging process

   c. prior to charging   d. air does not need to be purged

63. For recovery using the system's compressor, the recovery bottle should be connected to

 the manifold set...

   a. blue hose.   b. yellow hose.

   c. red hose.   d. gray hose.

64. When is it best to purge air out of the hoses when recovering a system?

   a. air does not need to be purged   b. prior to recovery

   c. when recovery is finished   d. during the recovery process

65. Opening the low side handle while charging connects...

   a. all three hoses.   b. the yellow and blue hose.

   c. the blue and red hose.   d. the yellow and red hose.

66. Opening the high side handle during recovery connects...

   a. all three hoses.   b. the yellow and blue hose.

   c. the blue and red hose.   d. the yellow and red hose.

67. On a 4 port manifold gauge set, which hose is the service hose?

    a. the middle 1/4" yellow hose   b. the middle 3/8" yellow hose

    c. the red hose   d. the blue hose

68. On a 4 port manifold gauge set, which hose is the vacuum hose?

    a. the middle 1/4" yellow hose   b. the middle 3/8" yellow hose

    c. the red hose   d. the blue hose

Fill in the blanks with the correct word(s).

69. Digital manifold sets have many different refrigerant _____

_____ built into them.

70. Some digital manifold sets are equipped with temp sensors that allow _____ and

_____ calculations to be performed automatically which the system is running.

71. Digital and compound manifold gauge sets must be checked prior to connecting to a system to ensure

that the _____ reading is zero.

72. Temp readers and sensors must be checked and _____ to ensure

accurate measurements and readings.

73. What are two types of temp reading sensors? _____ , _____

Use the P/T chart (Figure 4-8 found on page 40 of the textbook) to answer the following questions:

74. What is the saturated temp of R-22 at 84 PSIG? _____ °F

75. What is the saturated temp of R-410A at 170 PSIG? _____ °F

76. What is the saturated temp of R-410A at 365 PSIG? _____ °F

77. If R-22 saturated refrigerant is at a pressure of 168 PSIG, what temp should it be? _____ °F

78. If R-410A saturated refrigerant is at a pressure of 118 PSIG, what temp should it be? _____ °F

79. If R-410A saturated refrigerant is at a pressure of 295 PSIG, what temp should it be? _____ °F

80. If an unlabeled recovery bottle pressure is 185 PSIG in a 65° F room, what refrigerant is inside the bottle?

_____

Use each image to solve the following questions.

81. What is the pressure measured on each gauge?

    a. Blue Low Side Gauge _____ PSIG

    b. Red High Side Gauge _____ PSIG

82. What is the **R-410A** saturated temp measured on each gauge?

    a. Blue Low Side Gauge _____ °F

    b. Red High Side Gauge _____ °F

83. What is the **R-410A** saturated temp measured on each gauge?

    a. Blue Low Side Gauge _____ °F

    b. Red High Side Gauge _____ °F

84. What is the **R-22** saturated temp measured on each gauge?

    a. Blue Low Side Gauge _____ °F

    b. Red High Side Gauge _____ °F

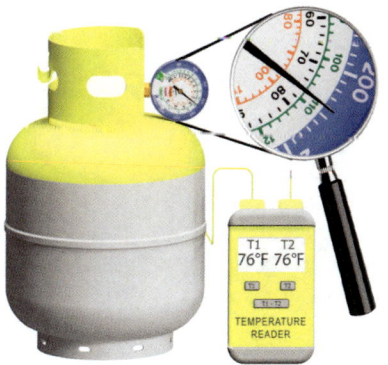

85. What refrigerant is in the recovery

    bottle, <u>R-410A</u> or <u>R-22</u>?

    _____

86. What refrigerant is in the recovery

    bottle, <u>R-410A</u> or <u>R-22</u>?

    _____

87. What refrigerant is in this off and equalized system, <u>R-22</u> or <u>R410A</u>?

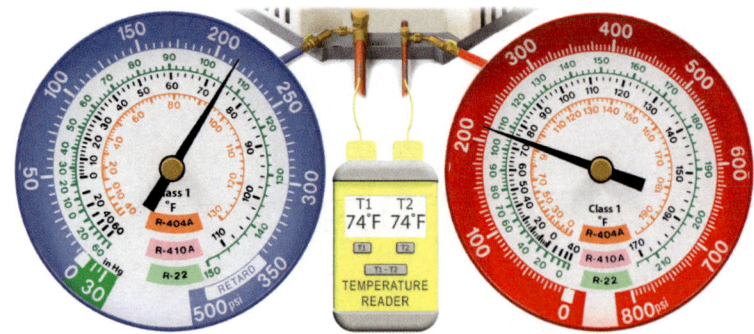

_____

88. What refrigerant is in this off and equalized system, <u>R-22</u> or <u>R410A</u>?

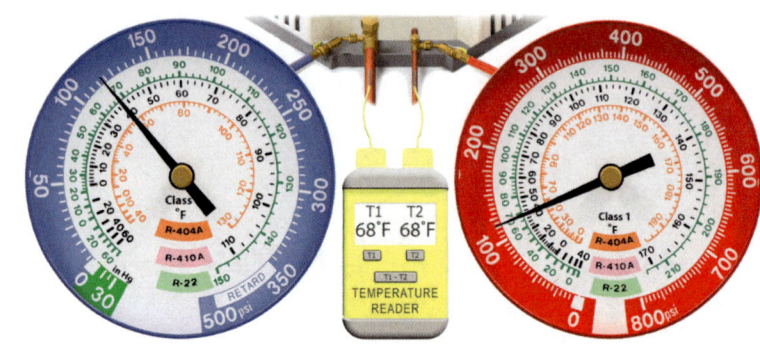

_____

89. Does this image depict <u>charging</u> or <u>recovering</u> while connected to a running system?

_____

90. Does this image depict <u>charging</u> or <u>recovering</u> while connected to a running system?

_____

CHAPTER 5
Service Access Ports

Fill in the blanks with the correct word(s).

1. Prior to and while accessing a system's refrigerant charge, *always* wear safety

   _____, butyl lined _____, and other PPE.

2. While accessing a system's refrigerant charge **always** have _____

   _____ available or wear _____.

3. **Never** breathe in _____ _____.

4. PPE stands for Personal _____ _____.

5. SCBA stands for _____ _____ Breathing _____.

6. Technicians must have the appropriate EPA 608 _____ prior to working on a

   _____ based system or buying refrigerant.

7. EPA safety guidelines can be found through this website: _____.

Match the left hand column items with those in the right hand column.

8. _____ A temporary clamp-on access port...

9. _____ A permanent access port will need...

10. _____ The valve core allows access...

11. _____ A clamp-on piercing access port is not usually used as a permanent port due...

12. _____ Bolt-on piercing access ports come in a variety of sizes...

13. _____ Make sure to first clean the outside of the tube...

a. to fit snugly around each different tube size.

b. to the refrigerant charge and seals itself shut when the refrigerant hose is disconnected.

c. before installing the piercing access tool.

d. can be installed for the initial service and recovery.

e. to be installed prior to adding refrigerant back into the system.

f. to the potential for future leaks at the seal.

Circle T for True or F for False.

14. **T / F** In order to read system pressure, connect the gauge hose end to the access port.

15. **T / F** Service valves allow refrigerant to be locked in the metering device of a split system.

16. **T / F** Service valves do not allow for a pump down of the system.

17. **T / F** Window air conditioners, portable stand up air conditioners, refrigerators, freezers and trailer air conditioners all have access ports.

18. **T / F** In order to service the refrigerant charge of a system without ports, access ports must be installed.

19. **T / F** A thumb screw valve depressor is used to remove the valve core.

20. **T / F** A valve core allows access to the inside of the port.

21. **T / F** A valve core keeps the port open when the refrigerant hose is disconnected.

22. **T / F** Valve core removal tools should be connected to the ports when checking the refrigerant charge.

23. **T / F** Valve core removal tools should be connected to the ports prior to recovering all the refrigerant from a system.

24. **T / F** A refrigerant hose should always be equipped with a low loss fitting on the end.

25. **T / F** A valve core removal tool cannot be used to replace a faulty valve core while a system is under pressure.

26. **T / F** On the end of the refrigerant hose, a valve core depressor is needed to access the refrigerant charge of a system with a three-position service valve.

27. **T / F** Locking valve caps must be used on all exposed refrigerant ports.

28. **T / F** A proper location to install an access port is on the process stub.

Answer the following with complete sentences.

29. What is the purpose of a port cap? _____

_____

_____

30. Some metal port caps have an O-ring inside and some do not. Describe the shape/design of the metal caps that **do not** have an O-ring. _____

_____

31. Why do technicians need a variety of keys to unlock valve caps? _____

_____

_____

32. Why should hoses with low loss fittings be used to check the refrigerant charge?

_____

_____

_____

CHAPTER 6
Service Valves

Circle the best answer for each statement/question.

1. The three-position service valve is used in refrigeration systems to...

    a. gain access to the ports.   b. perform a pump down.

    c. to service the system.   d. All of the above

2. The three-position service valve located on the top or side of the receiver is also known as the...

    a. King Valve.   b. Main Valve.

    c. Key Valve.   d. All of the above

3. The best tool for changing the positions of the valve in a three position service valve is the...

    a. ratcheting service wrench.   b. pair of locking pliers.

    c. valve core removal tool.   d. locking cap multi-tool.

Match the left hand column items with those in the right hand column.

4. _____ Back-Seat   a. All three pathways are connected. This is used to measure pressure or to adjust the refrigerant charge while the system is running.

5. _____ Front-Seat   b. The service port is closed off and the other two pathways are connected.

6. _____ Mid-Seat   c. The stem is turned clockwise all the way down until it stops.

Fill in the blanks with the correct word(s).

7. A three-position refrigeration service valve differs from one that is used on air conditioning and heat pump units due to the _____ being connected to different parts of the system.

8. When the outdoor unit of a split system is shipped with refrigerant, the valves are _____-Seated.

9. _____-Seat is when the stem is turned counterclockwise all the way up.

10. Mid-Seat can refer to positioning the stem halfway downward from the Back-Seat position when the system's power is off for _____ and _____.

11. _____-Seat is when the stem is turned _____ all the way down until it stops.

12. The valves are _____-Seated when the system is running and the gauge hoses are not connected to the ports.

Put the following steps in order to <u>connect</u> the refrigerant hose to the service port of a three position service valve.

13. _____ Step One:

14. _____ Step Two:

15. _____ Step Three:

16. _____ Step Four:

a. Make sure the manifold gauge set handles are shut and connect the refrigerant hose to the port.

b. Mid-Seat the stem to take a refrigerant pressure reading.

c. Take the top stem cap off.

d. Make sure the valve is Back-Seated before removing the side service port cap.

Put the following steps in order to <u>disconnect</u> a refrigerant hose from the service port of a three position service valve.

17. _____ Step One:

18. _____ Step Two:

19. _____ Step Three:

20. _____ Step Four:

a. Disconnect the hose from the port.

b. Install the port cap and the stem cap.

c. Back-Seat the stem on the service valve.

d. Leak check the port with bubble leak detector and then blow out the leak detector.

Match the left hand column items with those in the right hand column.

21. _____ The two position service valve is currently...

22. _____ The two position service valve has a Front-Seat position but does not technically have...

23. _____ The two position service valve has...

24. _____ When opening the two position valve with a service wrench and hex adapter,...

25. _____ A hex adapter is used to move...

a. the stem of a two position service valve.

b. do not force the stem upwards all the way up.

c. a valve core located in the service port.

d. a Back-Seat position.

e. the most common service valve used in air conditioning.

Circle T for True or F for False.

26. **T / F** When a two position service valve is Fully Open, the valve core seals the port which stops the pressure from escaping.

27. **T / F** When a two position service valve is Front-Seated, it shuts off the pathway of the indoor unit from the line set and port.

28. **T / F** When a two position service valve is Front-Seated, the line set and service port remain connected.

29. **T / F** The three position service valve is similar to the two position service valve in that they both have a valve core at the service port.

Label the service valve as either a three position service valve or a two position service valve.

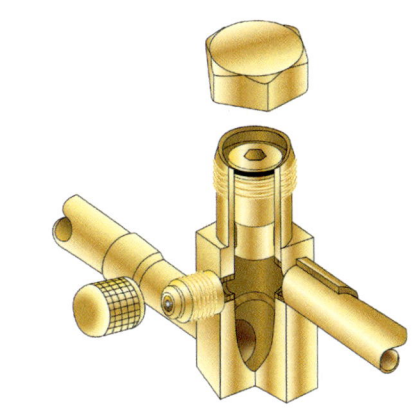

30. _____

31. _____

Label each service valve position as <u>Front-Seat</u>, <u>Mid-Seat</u>, or <u>Back-Seat</u>.

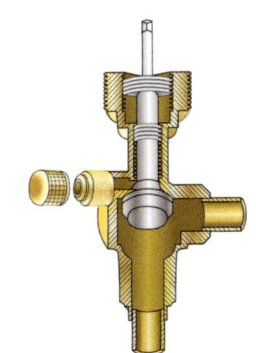

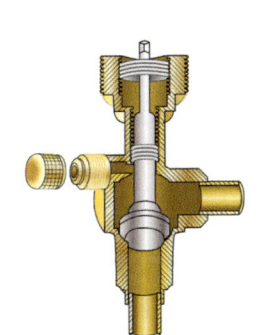

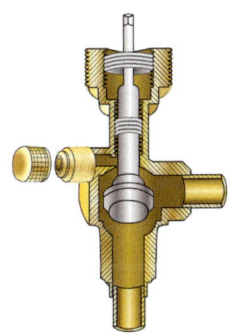

32. _____

33. _____

34. _____

Label the service valve position as either <u>Fully Open</u> or <u>Front-Seat</u>.

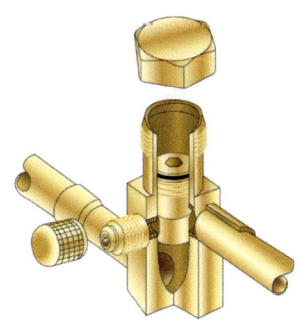

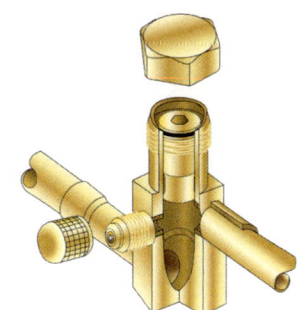

35. _____

36. _____

CHAPTER 7
Checking the Refrigerant Charge

Circle T for True or F for False.

1. **T / F** "Checking the refrigerant charge" refers to measuring a system's refrigerant charge using an approved method.

2. **T / F** Determining the refrigerant level is the only reason to "check the refrigerant charge".

3. **T / F** "Checking the charge" should only be done by using subcooling, total superheat, the total weight method, or other manufacturer recommended methods.

4. **T / F** To check the total superheat and subcooling of an air conditioner, the system must be on and both the indoor and outdoor temperatures must be 60° F or above.

5. **T / F** Before checking the refrigerant charge, check that the indoor return air filter is clean and sufficient airflow is moving across the indoor coil.

Fill in the blanks with the correct word(s).

6. Before starting up the unit in cooling mode to check the charge, connect the _____ _____ set to the system.

7. If the unit has a _____ metering device, the system must run for at least 5-10 minutes before measuring the subcooling.

8. If the unit has a _____ _____ metering device, the system must run for at least 10-15 minutes before measuring the total superheat.

9. Monitor the system's _____ during the initial start-up period.

10. If the vapor _____ _____ does not rise above 32° F, there may be a problem such as a low refrigerant charge, a liquid line restriction, or low airflow.

Circle the best answer for each statement/question.

11. The subcooling method is a refrigerant charging method used on...

    a. residential air conditioning units.   b. heat pumps.

    c. split systems.   d. All of the above

12. Two speed units are typically charged while...

    a. in both first and second speed.   b. in the first speed.

    c. in the second speed.   d. All of the above

13. In order to find the subcooling, both the saturated temperature of the refrigerant in the condenser and the actual temperature of the liquid refrigerant _____ must be known.

    a. entering the condenser
    b. exiting the condenser

    c. exiting the compressor
    d. None of the above

14. The pressure in the middle of the condenser is the same as the pressure at the...

    a. vapor line port on the outdoor unit.
    b. TXV.

    c. liquid line port on the outdoor unit.
    d. None of the above

15. What can be used to convert the pressure in the middle of the condenser to saturated temperature?

    a. a P/T chart
    b. a P/T app

    c. the P/T gauge built on the gauge face
    d. All of the above

Answer the following with complete sentences.

16. What is subcooling? _____

_____

17. Why must the actual subcooling be compared to the target subcooling? _____

_____

18. Where are the two most likely places the manufacturer's recommended subcooling can be found on an outdoor unit? _____

_____

_____

19. Why is it important to get the actual subcooling as close as possible to the target subcooling?

_____

_____

_____

20. On the line below, write the equation for finding subcooling.

_____

Fill in the blanks with the correct word(s).

21. Subcooling is used to check the charge of systems with a _____ metering device.

22. Read the subcooling via the _____ side gauge and the _____ line.

23. If the actual subcooling is less than the target subcooling do this to the system: _____ refrigerant.

24. If the actual subcooling is more than the target subcooling do this to the system: _____ refrigerant.

25. If the actual subcooling is within a range of 3° F more or 3° F less than the target subcooling do this to the system: _____

26. If the rating plate is worn off and the target subcooling cannot be determined, it is best to use a target subcooling of _____ ° F.

Match the left hand column items with those in the right hand column.

27. _____ Confirm the proper heat transfer at the indoor coil by...

28. _____ Delta T is...

29. _____ A single speed air conditioning system with a correct refrigerant charge, correct airflow, and a TXV metering device...

30. _____ Very high humidity in the conditioned air inside a building may...

a. should have a Delta T of about 18-21° F.

b. prevent a Delta T of 18-21° F from being reached.

c. measuring the Delta T.

d. the temperature decrease of the air as it moves across the evaporator.

Circle the correct bold term(s).

31. Delta T is found by measuring the air temperature a few feet upstream from the evaporator coil in the **return / supply** duct and a few feet downstream from the evaporator coil in the **return / supply** duct.

32. The TXV will somewhat compensate for high or low airflow by trying to maintain a steady **Delta T / superheat**.

33. The **total superheat / total weight** method is used to check the charge during air conditioning mode of systems that have a **fixed orifice / TXV** as the metering device.

34. Total superheat is found by taking the **actual / sat** temp on the large vapor line minus the **actual / sat** temp on the low pressure side of the system.

35. To use the total superheat method to check the refrigerant charge, the outdoor unit must be a **one / two** speed model and the outdoor and indoor air temps must both be at or above **70° / 90°** F.

Circle T for True or F for False.

36. **T / F** Total superheat is the temperature increase of the refrigerant from where the refrigerant comes out of the saturated state as a complete liquid in the evaporator until it enters the vapor service port of the outdoor unit.

37. **T / F** Superheat is the temperature increase in the vapor refrigerant above the temperature of it's saturation point.

38. **T / F** Compressor safety can be determined by measuring total superheat since the port is usually right before the compressor.

39. **T / F** The compressor is designed to handle both liquid and vapor refrigerant entering it.

40. **T / F** Total superheat can be used to verify that the refrigerant level is correct in a system with a fixed orifice metering device.

Circle the best answer for each statement/question.

41. To get an accurate refrigerant charge within a system, which of these should match the target superheat?

a. the target subcooling

b. the total superheat

c. the indoor DB temp

d. the vapor line temp

42. The target superheat is determined by measuring which of these?

a. the temperature at the inlets to the compressor and condenser

b. the liquid and the vapor temps near the compressor

c. the outdoor wet bulb temp and the indoor dry bulb temp

d. the outdoor dry bulb temp and the indoor wet bulb temp

43. Which of these tools will not measure the wet bulb (WB) temp?

a. a temp reader with a wet sock over the temp sensor

b. a temp reader with two temp sensors

c. a sling psychrometer

d. a digital psychrometer

44. Which of these would not help you find the target superheat for a system after you input the WB and DB temps into it?

a. a sling psychrometer

b. a target superheat chart

c. a calculator with formula

d. a written formula

45. To measure the indoor WB temp, the measurement must be taken at least 2 feet...

a. upstream from the condenser.

b. downstream from the evaporator coil.

c. upstream from the evaporator coil.

d. upstream from the condenser.

Circle the correct bold term(s).

46. The most accurate WB temp reading is taken two feet **before / after** the evaporator coil in the **return / supply** duct.

47. Measure the OA temp about one foot away from the **building / outdoor unit** and away from the hot discharge air of the outdoor fan.

48. To use the target superheat chart on page 75 of the textbook, find where the horizontal line from the outdoor **DB /WB** intersects the vertical line from indoor **DB / WB** temp in order to determine the target superheat.

49. Actual Total Superheat > Target Superheat = **Add / Recover** Refrigerant

50. Actual Total Superheat < Target Superheat = **Add / Recover** Refrigerant

Match the left hand column items with those in the right hand column.

51. _____ Delta T

a. Method used to check the charge on systems that have a TXV

52. _____ Target superheat

b. Method used to check the charge on systems that have a fixed orifice metering device

53. _____ Total superheat

c. The best superheat for the system to be set to

54. _____ Outdoor ambient temp

d. Tool for measuring the WB temp

55. _____ Psychrometer

e. The temp decrease of the air as it crosses the evaporator

56. _____ Subcooling

f. The temp of the air entering the outdoor unit

Circle T for True or F for False.

57. **T / F** If the actual superheat is higher than the target superheat, the system is overcharged.

58. **T / F** If the actual superheat and target superheat show that the system is overcharged, refrigerant needs to be recovered from the system.

59. **T / F** Refrigerant needs to be recovered from the system if the actual total superheat is lower that the target superheat.

60. **T / F** The Delta T needs to be taken across the vapor and liquid line during cooling mode in order to verify that the system is exchanging heat properly.

61. **T / F** During cooling mode, a TXV is able to allow more refrigerant than a fixed orifice into the evaporator coil to absorb the high humidity and heat from within a building.

62. **T / F** When the temperature within the building is high during the initial startup of a system with a fixed orifice metering device, the Delta T will nearly always read between 18-21° F.

63. **T / F** Total Superheat = Actual Temp on the vapor line – Saturated Temp from the vapor line

Use the target superheat chart (Figure 7-9 on page 75 of the textbook) to solve the following problems.

64. What is the target superheat when the WB temp = 68° F and the DB temp = 95° F? _____ ° F

65. What is the target superheat when the WB temp = 58° F and the DB temp = 75° F? _____ ° F

Use the target superheat equation (found on page 74 of the textbook) to solve the following questions.

Remember that results from the equation may differ slightly from the Target Superheat Chart.

66. What is the target superheat when the WB temp = 66° F and the DB temp = 90° F? Show all work.

_____

_____

67. What is the target superheat when the WB temp = 62° F and the DB temp = 80° F? Show all work.

_____

_____

_____

Answer the following with complete sentences.

68. Regardless of the charging method, why must the vapor saturated temp stay above 32° F?

_____

_____

_____

69. When checking the refrigerant charge using the Total Superheat method, why must the indoor WB temp and Outdoor DB temp continually be remeasured?

_____

_____

_____

Circle T for True or F for False.

70. **T / F** Always check for a clean air filter and proper airflow volume prior to checking the refrigerant charge.

71. **T / F** The indoor and outdoor temps must be 80° F or higher before checking the charge.

72. **T / F** Wait 5 minutes before checking the charge on a system with a fixed orifice metering device.

73. **T / F** Verify that the low side sat temp remains above 32° F.

74. **T / F** Check the refrigerant charge level in subcooling using the red high side gauge and a temp sensor on the vapor line within 3 inches of the service port.

75. **T / F** Find the target subcooling by measuring the indoor WB temp and outdoor DB temp.

76. **T / F** The target superheat is listed on the outdoor unit rating plate.

Circle the best answer for each statement/question.

77. Refrigerant must be recovered from the system when...

    a. actual superheat < target superheat.   b. actual superheat > target superheat.

    c. actual superheat +/- 2° F of target superheat.   d. None of the above

78. The refrigerant level in the system is correct when...

    a. actual superheat < target superheat.   b. actual superheat > target superheat.

    c. actual superheat +/- 2° F of target superheat.   d. None of the above

79. Refrigerant must be added to the system when...

    a. actual superheat < target superheat.   b. actual superheat > target superheat.

    c. actual superheat +/- 2° F of target superheat.   d. None of the above

80. The refrigerant level in the system is correct when...

    a. actual subcooling < target subcooling.   b. actual subcooling > target subcooling.

    c. actual subcooling +/- 3° F of target subcooling.   d. None of the above

Fill in the blanks with the correct word(s).

81. The total weight method is the process of breaking the _____ of an empty system with the _____ _____ of refrigerant needed for the system.

82. The total refrigerant weight is usually listed on the rating plate as the _____ _____.

83. An _____ _____ must be used to weigh in the refrigerant when using the total weight method.

84. On a _____ _____, the factory charge is the exact amount of refrigerant needed to allow the system to work properly.

Define the Following

85. Packaged unit:

_____

86. Split System:

_____

_____

87. Mini-split:

_____

_____

_____

Use the Refrigerant Weight Per Foot Guide (Figure 7-13 on page 83 of the textbook) to answer the following questions.

88. An R-410A split system heat pump is installed with 50' of 3/8" liquid line and 50' of 7/8" vapor line. The manufacturer's factory charge of 8 lb 5 oz includes enough refrigerant for 15' of 3/8" and 15' of 7/8" line set. How much extra refrigerant needs to be <u>added</u> to the factory charge? Show all your work.

89. An R-410A split system heat pump is installed with 10' of 3/8" liquid line and 10' of 3/4" vapor line. The manufacturer's factory charge of 6 lb 2 oz includes enough refrigerant for 25' of 3/8" and 25' of 3/4" line set. How much refrigerant needs to be <u>recovered</u> from the factory charge? Show all your work.

90. An R-407C split system air conditioner is installed with 55' of 3/8" liquid line and 55' of 3/4" vapor line. The manufacturer's factory charge of 7 lb 4 oz includes enough refrigerant for 25' of 3/8" and 25' of 3/4" line set. How much refrigerant needs to be <u>added</u> to the factory charge? Show all your work.

Use each image to solve the following questions.

91. Using this image of an outdoor unit rating plate, what is the target subcooling?

    Target subcooling: _____

92. Using the indoor WB temp and the outdoor DB temp from this image, along with the target superheat chart (Figure 7-9 on page 75 of the textbook), what is the target superheat?

    Target superheat: _____

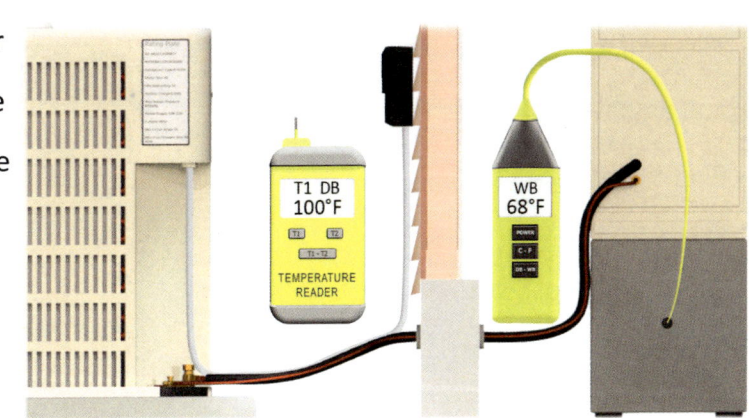

93. Using the indoor WB temp and the outdoor DB temp from this image, along with the target superheat chart (Figure 7-9 on page 75 of the textbook), what is the target superheat?

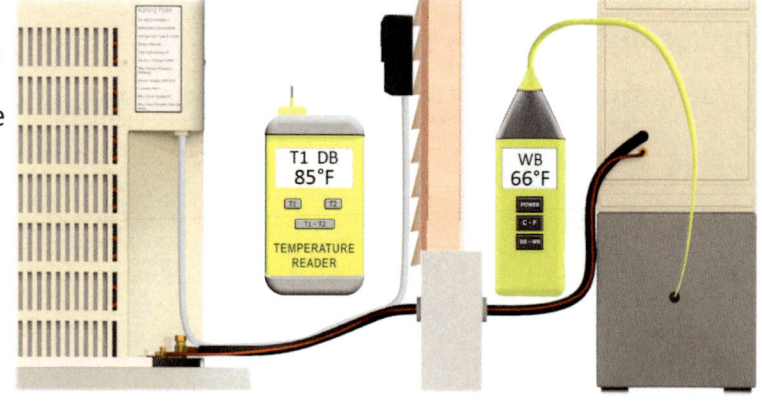

Target superheat: _____

94. Determine the actual total superheat and actual subcooling from this image of a running **R-410A** unit.

a. Actual Total Superheat: _____

b. Actual Subcooling: _____

95. Determine the actual total superheat and actual subcooling from this image of a running **R-410A** unit.

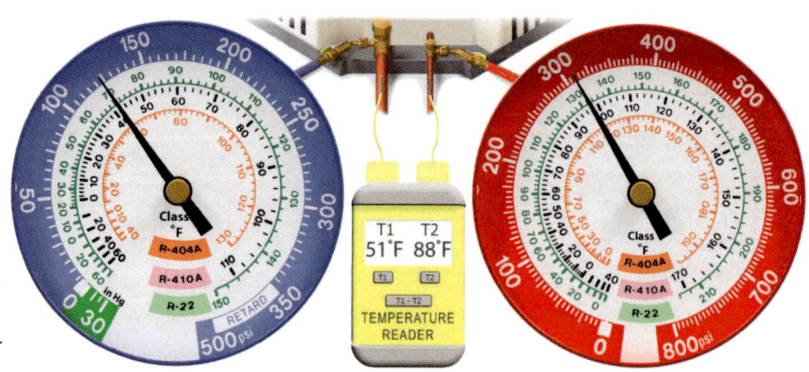

a. Actual Total Superheat: _____

b. Actual Subcooling: _____

96. Determine the actual total superheat and actual subcooling from this image of a running **R-22** unit.

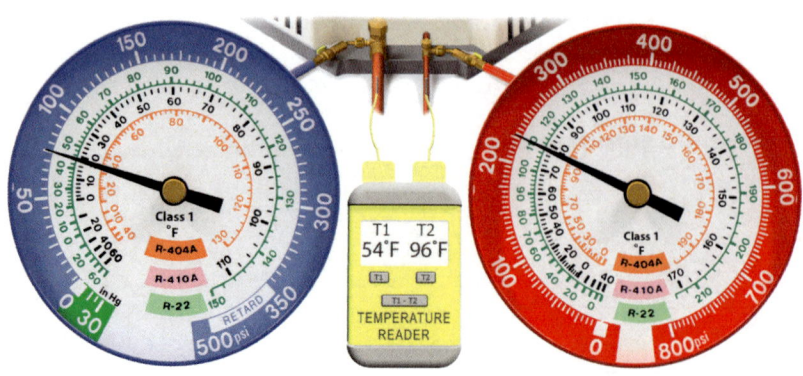

a. Actual Total Superheat: _____

b. Actual Subcooling: _____

97. Determine the actual total superheat and actual subcooling from this image of a running **R-22** unit.

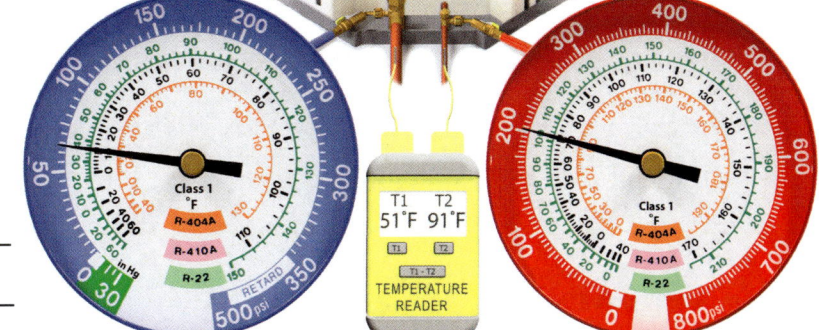

    a. Actual Total Superheat: _____

    b. Actual Subcooling: _____

98. Determine if the unit is underchanged, correct charge, or overcharged by measuring the actual total superheat and actual subcooling from this image of a running **R-410A** unit with a **piston metering device**.

Target Superheat: 18° F

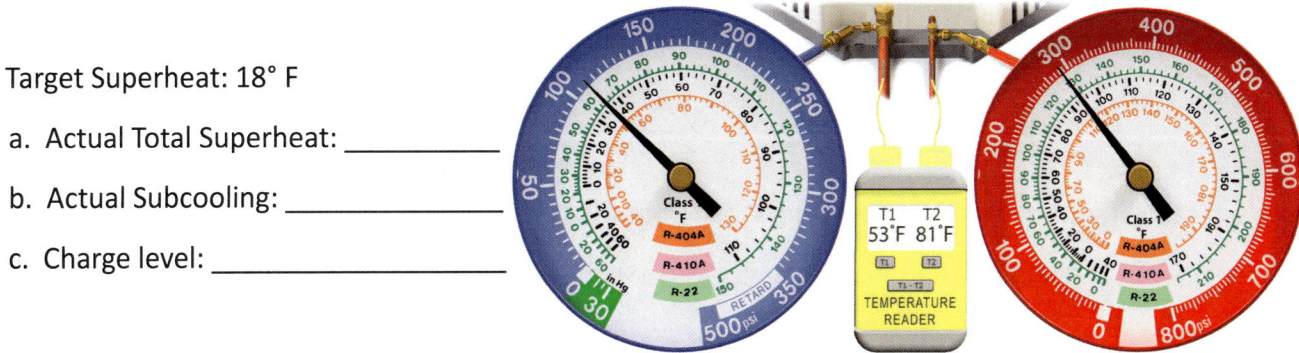

    a. Actual Total Superheat: _____

    b. Actual Subcooling: _____

    c. Charge level: _____

99. Determine if the unit is undercharged, correct charge, or overcharged by measuring the actual total superheat and actual subcooling from this image of a running **R-410A** unit with a **TXV metering device**.

Target Subcooling: 13° F

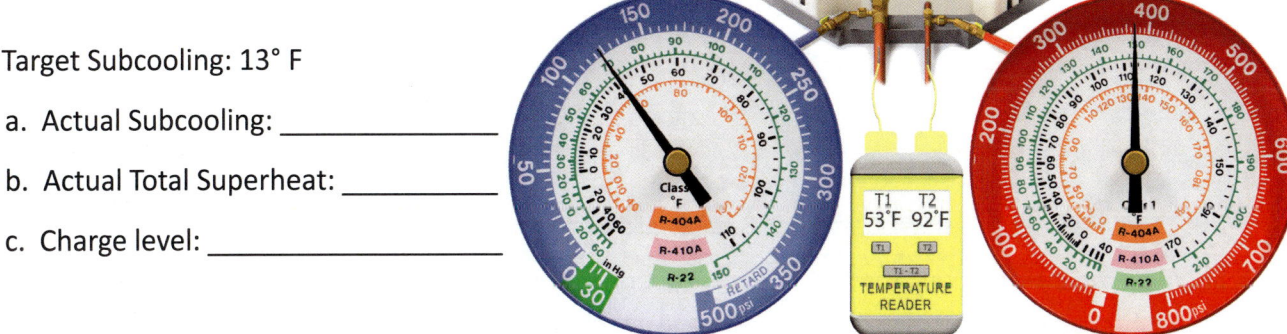

    a. Actual Subcooling: _____

    b. Actual Total Superheat: _____

    c. Charge level: _____

100. Determine if the unit is undercharged, correct charge, or overcharged by measuring the actual total superheat and actual subcooling from this image of a running **R-22** unit with a **piston metering device**.

Target Superheat: 19° F

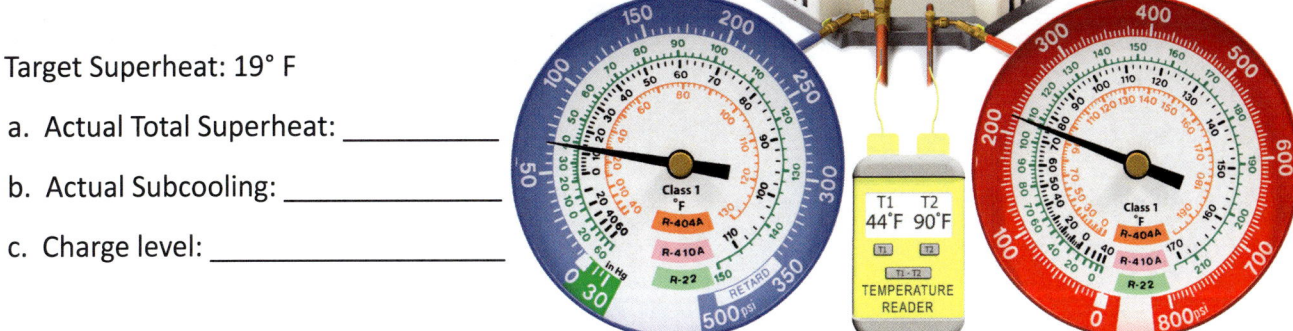

    a. Actual Total Superheat: _____

    b. Actual Subcooling: _____

    c. Charge level: _____

101. Determine if the unit is <u>overcharged</u>, <u>correct charge</u>, or <u>undercharged</u> by measuring the actual total superheat, and actual subcooling from this image of a running **R-410A** unit with a **TXV metering device**.

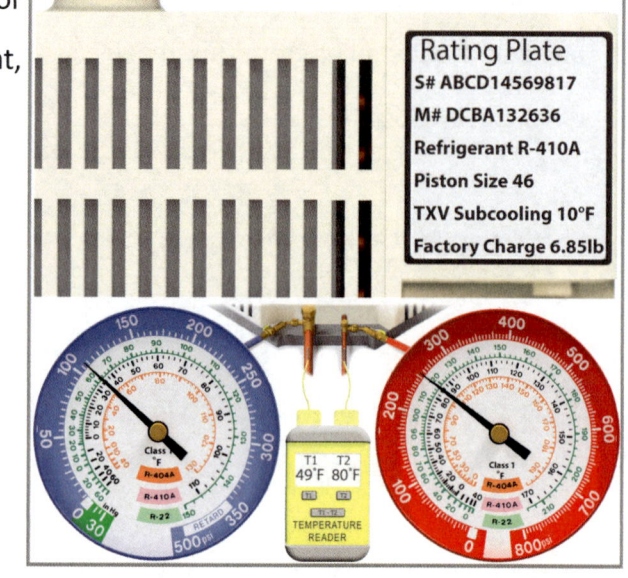

   a. Target Subcooling: _____

   b. Actual Subcooling: _____

   c. Actual Total Superheat: _____

   d. Charge Level: _____

102. Determine if the unit is <u>overcharged</u>, <u>correct charge</u>, or <u>undercharged</u> by measuring the actual target superheat, actual total superheat, and actual subcooling from this image of a running **R-410A** unit with a **piston metering device**.

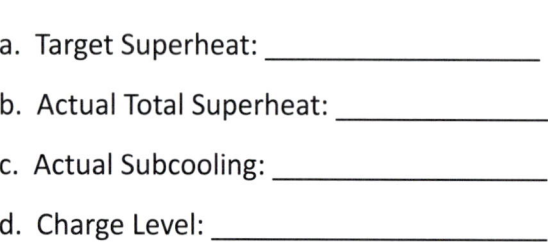
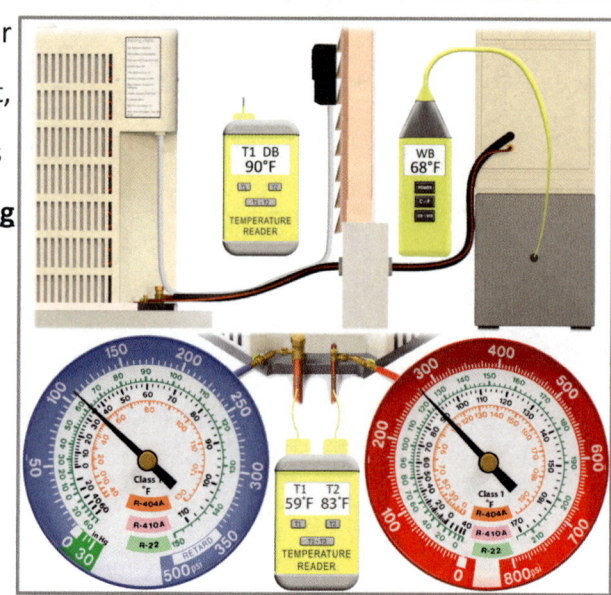

   a. Target Superheat: _____

   b. Actual Total Superheat: _____

   c. Actual Subcooling: _____

   d. Charge Level: _____

103. Determine if the unit is <u>overcharged</u>, <u>correct charge</u>, or <u>undercharged</u> by measuring the actual target superheat, actual total superheat, and actual subcooling from this image of a running **R-22** unit with a **piston metering device**.

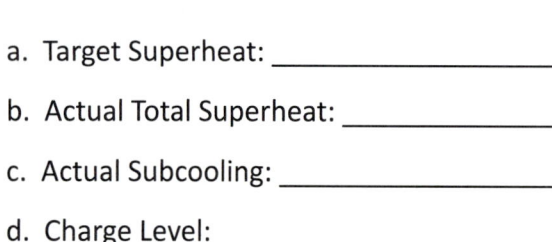
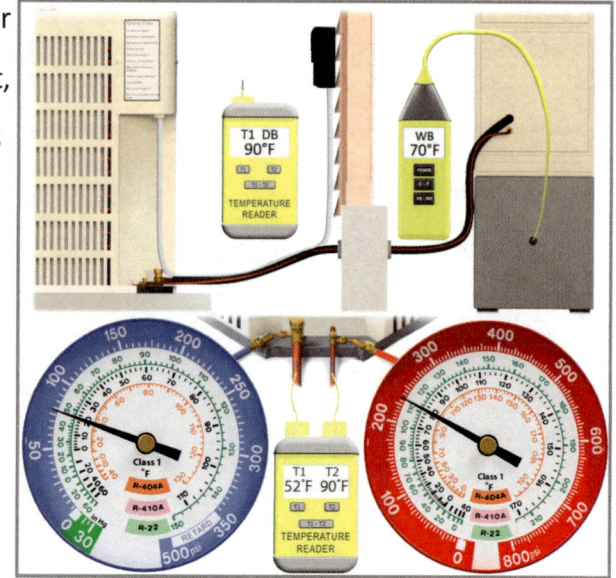

   a. Target Superheat: _____

   b. Actual Total Superheat: _____

   c. Actual Subcooling: _____

   d. Charge Level: _____

CHAPTER 8
Charging and Recovery of Refrigerant

Circle T for True or F for False.

1. **T / F** While accessing a system's refrigerant charge, the use of Personal Protective Equipment (PPE) is not necessary.

2. **T / F** To connect the blue hose to the center yellow hose, turn the high side handle on the manifold gauge set counterclockwise.

3. **T / F** To connect the red hose to the center yellow hose, turn the low side handle on the manifold gauge set counterclockwise.

4. **T / F** If both the low side and high side handles of the manifold gauge set are fully turned clockwise, all three hoses will be connected.

5. **T / F** The manifold gauge set handles should be closed while checking the charge of a running system.

Fill in the blanks with the correct word(s).

6. It is important to _____ _____ from the hoses prior to adding or recovering refrigerant from a running system.

7. If the system is running, make sure not to _____ both the low side and the high side handles at the same time.

8. If the system is _____ and equalized, purge air out of the red and blue refrigerant hoses at the same time through the yellow service hose end.

9. Close both handles on the manifold gauge set before turning the system on, otherwise liquid refrigerant will enter the _____ which may damage it.

10. An air conditioning system with a fixed orifice is low on refrigerant if the actual superheat is _____ than the target superheat.

11. An air conditioning system with a fixed orifice is overcharged with refrigerant if the actual superheat is _____ than the target superheat.

12. An air conditioning system with a TXV is overcharged with refrigerant if the actual subcooling is _____ than the target subcooling.

13. A heat pump with an active TXV metering device in cooling mode is low on refrigerant if the actual subcooling is _____ than the target subcooling.

Circle the best answer for each statement/question.

14. After determining a system is low on refrigerant,...

    a. add refrigerant.

    b. always sell a new system.

    c. find and fix any leaks, then add refrigerant.

    d. None of the above

15. If a disposable bottle is used to add refrigerant to a system, turn the bottle upside down to allow...

    a. a liquid & vapor refrigerant mixture to exit the bottle.

    b. liquid refrigerant to exit the bottle.

    c. vapor refrigerant to exit the bottle.

    d. the higher pressure refrigerant to exit the bottle.

16. If a disposable bottle containing a blend refrigerant is used to add refrigerant to a system, turn the bottle upside down to allow...

    a. the correct liquid mixture of component refrigerants to exit the bottle.

    b. each individual component refrigerant to exit the bottle separately.

    c. the correct vapor mixture of the component refrigerants to exit the bottle.

    d. None of the above

17. On a reusable refrigerant bottle, such as a recovery bottle,...

    a. the bottle should not be turned upside down to get the liquid out from the dip tube.

    b. open the red handle to connect the port to the dip tube in the bottle.

    c. Neither a nor b

    d. Both a and b

Circle the correct bold term(s).

18. **Liquid / Vapor** refrigerant is located toward the top of the refrigerant bottle when the bottle is upright.

19. In the case of a **blend / single** component refrigerant, charging can be performed with the bottle up right, while the system is running.

20. When charging refrigerant into a running system, the liquid or vapor refrigerant from the bottle is at a **higher / lower** pressure than the pressure in the low side of the system.

21. When charging refrigerant into a running system, the refrigerant must be added into the **high side liquid port / low side vapor port.**

22. While the system is running, the high side pressure of the system will be at a **higher / lower** pressure than the pressure within the bottle.

Circle T for True or F for False.

23. **T / F** Liquid refrigerant can be weighed into the empty system's liquid line while the system is both off and under vacuum.

24. **T / F** The small liquid line port is the low side during the cooling mode of a running system.

25. **T / F** During the cooling mode of a running system, if the small liquid line port is connected to a recovery bottle, the refrigerant will flow from the bottle into the system.

26. **T / F** A partial refrigerant charge can be recovered from a running system without having to turn off the system or connecting a recovery machine.

Fill in the blanks with the correct word(s).

27. While the system is _____, refrigerant can be weighed in a little at a time, as needed.

28. After _____ refrigerant, wait a few minutes before _____ the refrigerant charge. This must be done before adding in more refrigerant.

29. To increase subcooling, _____ refrigerant into the system.

30. While charging, do not allow too much refrigerant into the system each time the _____ gauge handle is opened on the manifold gauge set.

31. The system's vapor _____ can be damaged if _____ refrigerant enters it.

Match the left hand column items with those in the right hand column.

32. _____ If noise from the compressor changes...

33. _____ A compressor noise change may be an indication of...

34. _____ Let the new refrigerant cycle through...

35. _____ Check the new total superheat and subcooling...

a. before adding more refrigerant.

b. after the new refrigerant has cycled through.

c. stop adding refrigerant.

d. liquid slugging.

Circle the best answer for each statement/question.

36. An evaporator coil temperature below 32° F causes this to freeze onto the fins when it crosses the evaporator coil.

    a. air   b. humidity   c. nitrogen   d. refrigerant

37. What component can help phase change a refrigerant from liquid into a saturated state while charging?

    a. condenser   b. liquid vaporizer

    c. liquid solenoid   d. b and c

38. This must be measured continually while charging a system to make sure there is an accurate amount of refrigerant in the system.

    a. pressure   b. subcooling   c. superheat   d. b and c

39. Adding refrigerant...

    a. decreases the subcooling.   b. increases the subcooling.

    c. increases the superheat.   d. b and c

Circle the correct bold term(s).

40. An evaporator coil can develop frost due to a low refrigerant charge when the vapor saturated temperature is **above / below** 32° F.

41. The **compressor / indoor blower motor** in a split system can be turned off and on using the outdoor disconnect switch.

42. If the system has a **piston or capillary tubing / TXV** wait 5-10 minutes before checking the charge.

43. If the system has a **piston or capillary tubing / TXV,** wait 10-15 minutes before checking the charge.

44. Both the changing target superheat and the changing actual total superheat must be monitored at the same time when charging refrigerant into a system with a **fixed orifice / TXV.**

45. The WB temp inside the building will **lower / rise** while the system is running.

46. The actual total superheat will **lower / rise** after refrigerant is added into a system with a fixed orifice.

47. Monitor both the **target superheat / actual subcooling** and the actual total superheat until they line up as close as possible while charging.

48. Refrigerants such as CFC's, HCFC's, and HFC's **do / do not** require recovery.

Answer the following with complete sentences.

49. Define the term "recovery".

    _____

    _____

50. What is a "full recovery"?

    _____

    _____

51. The term *evacuation* can refer to what two procedures?

    _____

    _____

52. Which two methods can be used to recover refrigerant from a system? One can be used while the system is running and the other while the system is off. _____

_____

_____

List five precautions that must be taken when recovering refrigerant.

53. _____

54. _____

55. _____

56. _____

57. _____

Match the left hand column items with those in the right hand column.

58. _____ If a recovery bottle has air or other noncondesables mixed with the refrigerant inside the bottle,...

59. _____ Prior to use, a used recovery bottle's...

60. _____ If the system's compressor is used for recovery...

61. _____ The system's high side liquid pressure is higher than the pressure inside the...

62. _____ Before and during recovery to make sure the bottle does not get overfilled,...

63. _____ When a system's metering device is a TXV, the refrigerant charge must be...

a. checked with subcooling.

b. only a recovery bottle and a manifold gauge set are needed.

c. monitor the bottle's weight.

d. the pressure may be too high to use the system's compressor for recovery.

e. recovery bottle.

f. identification tag, neck, pressure and weight should be checked.

Circle T for True or F for False.

64. **T / F** Manual low loss or automatic quick disconnect fittings should be on the end of each hose.

65. **T / F** Before adding refrigerant to or recovering refrigerant from a running system, the disconnect procedure should be performed.

66. **T / F** The disconnect procedure ensures that an excessive amount of refrigerant is not lost from the system due to the manifold gauge set hoses being disconnected.

67. **T / F** Before performing the disconnect procedure, purge all the air from the red hose only. The blue hose never has air in it.

68. **T / F** The total superheat method of charging is used if the system has a TXV metering device.

69. **T / F** During the disconnect procedure, add the refrigerant from the yellow and red hose into the running system through the blue low side hose.

70. **T / F** The subcooling method of charging is used if the system has a TXV metering device.

71. **T / F** It is important not to overcharge the system when performing the disconnect procedure.

72. **T / F** Always leak check the ports prior to checking the refrigerant charge.

Circle the correct bold term(s).

73. Test gauges have a **long / short** stub which connects the gauge to the connection point.

74. The use of test gauges avoids having to purge **air / refrigerant** from the hoses.

75. The use of test gauges avoids having to **charge / recover** the liquid refrigerant from the hoses back into the system before disconnecting.

76. To verify that refrigerant is not leaking through the valve cores inside the **ports / hoses**, use a non-corrosive bubble leak detector to test for leaks.

77. If the ports are located in an accessible area, **locking / brass** caps must be installed on them to restrict **certified / unauthorized** individuals from accessing the ports.

78. If non-corrosive bubble leak detector is added directly to the ports, the leak detector must be **removed / left** prior to putting the caps back on.

Use the each image to solve the following questions.

79. Circle if the unit is <u>undercharged</u>, <u>correct charge</u>, or <u>overcharged</u> by measuring the target subcooling, actual total superheat and actual subcooling from this image of a running **R-410A** unit with a **TXV metering device**. Circle if the technician needs to <u>add</u> refrigerant, <u>recover</u> refrigerant, or take <u>no action</u>.

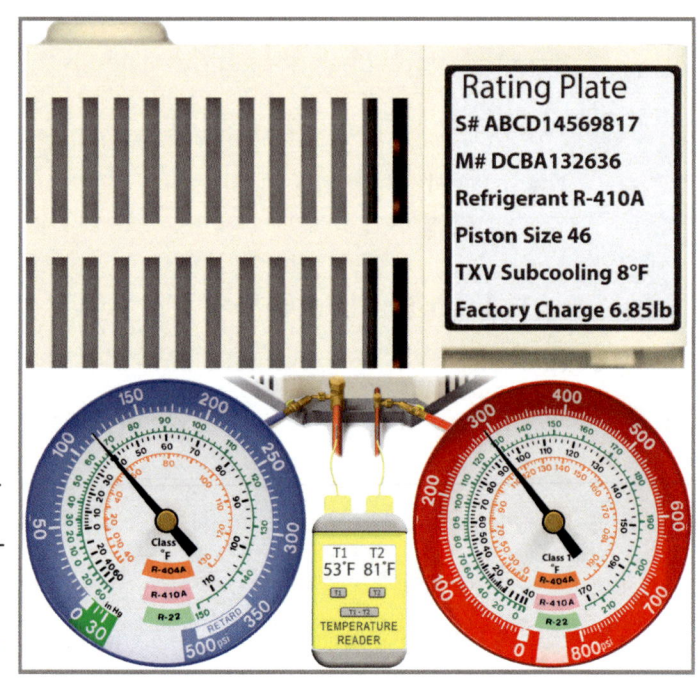

a. Target Subcooling: _____

b. Actual Subcooling: _____

c. Actual Total Superheat: _____

d. Charge: **undercharged / correct / overcharged**

e. Action: **add / no action / recover**

80. Circle if the unit is <u>undercharged</u>, <u>correct charge</u>, or <u>overcharged</u> by measuring the target superheat, actual total superheat and actual subcooling from this image of a running **R-410A** unit with a **piston metering device**. Circle if the technician needs to <u>add</u> refrigerant, <u>recover</u> refrigerant, or take <u>no action</u>.

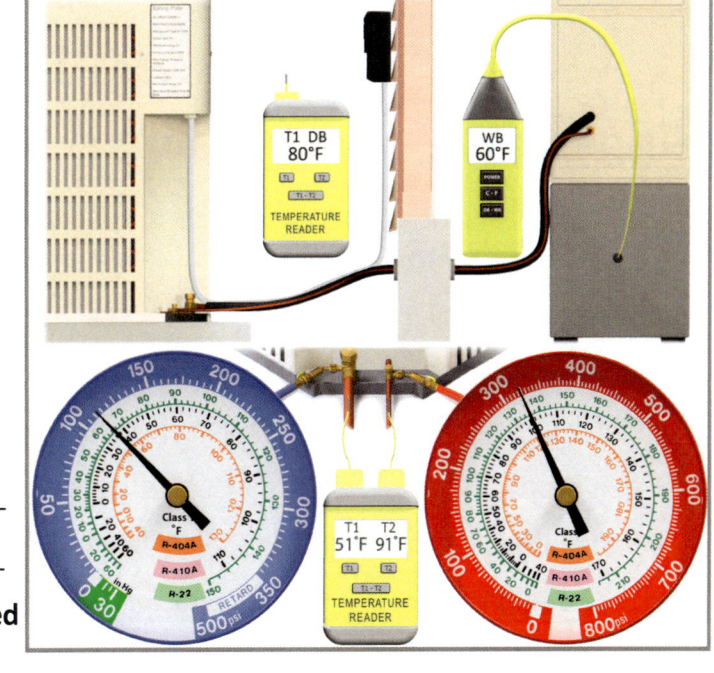

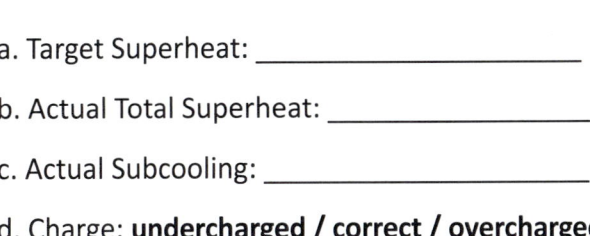

a. Target Superheat: _____

b. Actual Total Superheat: _____

c. Actual Subcooling: _____

d. Charge: **undercharged / correct / overcharged**

e. Action: **add / no action / recover**

81. Circle if the unit is <u>undercharged</u>, <u>correct charge</u>, or <u>overcharged</u> by measuring the target superheat, actual total superheat and actual subcooling from this image of a running **R-410A** unit with a **piston metering device**. Circle if the technician needs to <u>add</u> refrigerant, <u>recover</u> refrigerant, or take <u>no action</u>.

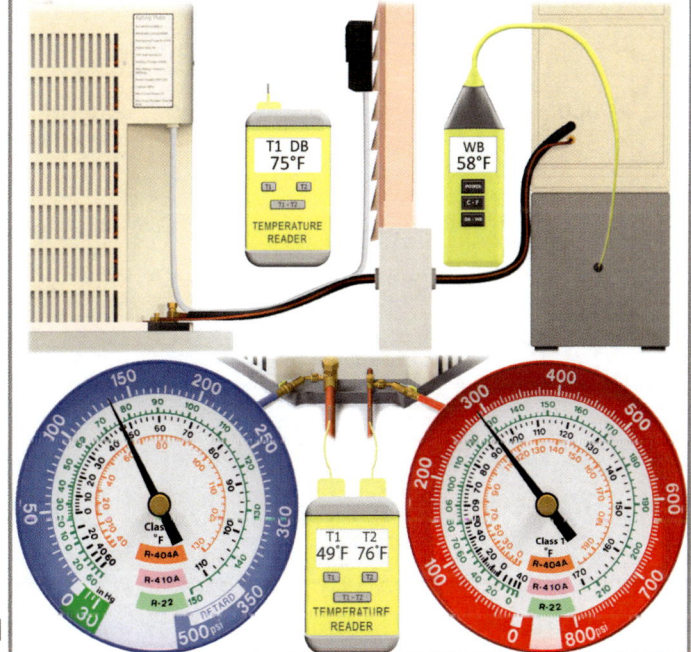

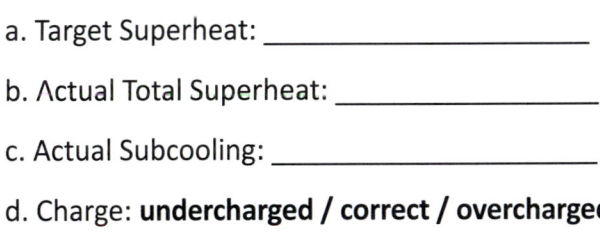

a. Target Superheat: _____

b. Actual Total Superheat: _____

c. Actual Subcooling: _____

d. Charge: **undercharged / correct / overcharged**

e. Action: **add / no action / recover**

CHAPTER 9

Refrigerant Recovery Machine Setup and Bottle Preparation

Circle T for True or F for False.

1. **T / F** A recovery bottle can be used to store more than one type of refrigerant at a time.

2. **T / F** There are two types of recovery bottles: "one time use" and "reusable".

3. **T / F** The liquid refrigerant in a reusable recovery bottle can be accessed by the dip tube on the red liquid port.

4. **T / F** The blue vapor port connects to the bottom of the bottle where the vapor is.

5. **T / F** A new recovery bottle is always ready for refrigerant without any preparation.

Fill in the blanks with the correct word(s).

6. A recovery bottle is usually shipped from the factory with _____ inside.

7. Vacuum a new recovery bottle to a level below _____ microns to prepare it for refrigerant.

8. Use a vacuum _____ and a vacuum _____ to perform the vacuum procedure on a recovery bottle.

9. After the vacuum reaches a level at or below the target, turn off the vacuum pump. Wait 10 minutes to see if the vacuum level rises. This is called the _____ _____ _____.

10. Recovery bottle information is stamped on the _____ of the bottle.

Answer the following.

11. What does it mean if the micron level stays below 500 microns during the standing vacuum test?

_____

12. What instrument/tool should be used to determine the amount of liquid in a used recovery bottle?

_____ _____

13. Why do some manufacturers or distributors set more stringent requirements than what is listed on the recovery bottle? _____

The following information can be found on a recovery bottle. What does each mean?

14. TW: _____   15. Max PSI: _____

16. WC: _____   17. Max Temp: _____

18. Date stamp: _____

Circle the best answer for each statement/question.

19. The total weight of a recovery bottle consists of...

    a. the bottle only.   b. the refrigerant inside the bottle.

    c. the TW and the refrigerant inside.   d. the liquid and vapor refrigerant.

20. The recovery bottle can be filled up to this percent of the WC.

    a. 80%   b. 85%   c. 90%   d. 95%

21. A recovery bottle with a WC of 47 lb or higher may be referred to as a...

    a. 45 lb bottle.   b. 50 lb bottle.   c. light use bottle.   d. All of the above

22. Which of these must not be exceeded in regards to a recovery bottle?

    a. maximum pressure rating   b. 80% WC

    c. maximum temperature rating   d. a, b and c

23. When a recovery bottle is not in use, it must be stored in area where the temp is _____ the max temp rating of the bottle.

    a. the same as   b. higher than

    c. lower than   d. All of the above

24. What is the usual max temp rating of a recovery bottle?

    a. 100° F   b. 110° F   c. 120° F   d. 130° F

Calculate the 80% allowable refrigerant capacity for these bottles. Show your work.

25. A recovery bottle with a WC of 46 lb = _____

26. A recovery bottle with a WC of 28 lb = _____

27. Use the information provided to find the maximum weight allowed for the recovery bottle. Show your work.

    *WC = 47 lb   *TW = 28 lb

    Max Weight allowed for the bottle and refrigerant = _____

28. Use the information provided to find the allowable capacity remaining inside a recovery bottle. Show your work.   *WC = 48 lb   *TW = 25 lb   *Actual total weight of recovery bottle = 55 lb

    Allowable refrigerant capacity remaining = _____

Circle T for True or F for False.

29. **T / F** Before and during the recovery process, an electronic scale should be used to measure the bottle's weight in order to avoid overfilling the bottle.

30. **T / F** The amount of refrigerant that is in a packaged air conditioner is listed on the rating plate as the *factory charge*.

31. **T / F** If the factory charge is more than the allowable capacity remaining in the bottle, it is safe to recover the full amount into the bottle.

32. **T / F** After a recovery bottle is filled to 90% of the WC, it should be exchanged for a new bottle of the same size.

33. **T / F** If a distributor finds two or more refrigerants mixed in a bottle, they may refuse to exchange the bottle or charge an extra fee.

34. **T / F** If a P/T chart is used to determine the type of refrigerant in a bottle, the bottle must be at a stable temp for at least several hours before measuring.

Circle the correct bold term(s).

35. It is important **to / not to** mix refrigerants in the same bottle.

36. It is important **to / not to** allow air or nitrogen in the bottle.

37. As long as there is **liquid / vapor** refrigerant in a bottle, the pressure will align to the saturated temp of the refrigerant as listed on a P/T chart.

38. The saturated temperature of the refrigerant in a bottle should be **similar to / different than** the temp on the outside of the bottle.

39. A **refrigerant analyzer / anemometer** can be used to determine the type of refrigerant in a bottle.

Fill in the blanks with the correct word(s).

40. Air can enter a recovery bottle through a loose _____ or through a _____ in the system during recovery.

41. A recovery bottle can become contaminated when the air is not _____ from the refrigerant hose setup prior to the recovery process.

42. If a recovery bottle has not been _____ prior to its first use, air may be in the bottle.

43. To avoid contamination, a recovery bottle should be marked with an _____ _____ that clearly states the type of refrigerant that is inside.

44. If refrigerant is going to be recovered from a system and charged back into the same owner's system, an _____ , _____ recovery bottle should be used.

Refrigerant Charging and Service Procedures for Air Conditioning

Workbook

ANSWER KEY

Chapter 1:
1. refrigerant
2. toxicity, flammability
3. a. Chlorine Fluorine Carbon
   b. Hydrogen Chlorine Fluorine Carbon
   c. Hydrogen Fluorine Carbon
4. a. HFC, b. HCFC, c. CFC
5. refrigeration
6. a. hydrofluoroolefin,
   b. hydrocarbon
7. flammable
8. R-290
9. $44,539
10. a. Ozone Depletion Potential
    b. Global Warming Potential
11. e
12. d
13. b
14. a
15. c
16. a and b
17. d
18. a
19. a
20. a
21. c
22. F
23: F
24. T
25. T
26. F
27. T
28. b and c
29. a
30. d
31. c
32. b
33. b
34. d
35. absorbs, reject
36. liquid, gas
37. EPA
38. British Thermal Unit
39. A BTU is the amount of heat added to 1lb of water to raise it 1˚ F (Fahrenheit).
40. d
41. b
42. a
43. c
44. saturated
45. lowers
46. pressure
47. saturated
48. evaporator, condenser
49. liquid, vapor
50. vapor, liquid
51. compressor, metering device

Chapter 2:
1. a. Vapor
   b. Vapor
   c. Compressor
   d. Condenser
   e. Evaporator
   f. Metering device
   g. Liquid
   h. Liquid
2. lower, heat
3. vapor, vapor
4. rejects
5. subcooled

Chapter 2 Continued:
6. a
7. c
8. b
9. b
10. d
11. c
12. a
13. f
14. e
15. g
16. h
17. b
18. T
19. T
20. T
21. F
22. T
23. F
24. filter drier
25. line set
26. receiver
27. metering device
28. reversing valve
29. accumulator
30: A TXV reduces or enlarges the orifice size depending on the heat load on the evaporator. A piston is a fixed orifice.
31: At the compressor inlet there is low pressure, low temperature, superheated vapor and at the compressor outlet there is high pressure and therefore, high temperature, superheated vapor.
32: At the inlet of the metering device there is high pressure, high temperature, subcooled liquid and at the outlet of the metering device there is low pressure, low temperature, subcooled liquid exiting.

Chapter 3:
1. a. TXV
   b. Indoor Evaporator Coil
   c. Filter Drier
   d. Outdoor Condensing Unit
   e. Compressor
   f. Forced Air Furnace with Blower Motor
   g. Condenser Coil
   h. Compressor Inlet
   i. Discharge Line
   j. Compressor Outlet
   k. Service Valve
2. four
3. three
4. five
5. one
6. two
7. eight
8. nine
9. six
10. ten
11. seven
12. thirteen
13. fourteen
14. fifteen
15. eleven
16. twelve
17. F
18. T
19. T
20. T

Chapter 3 Continued:
21. T
22. F
23. F
24. F
25. T
26. Subcooling is the temperature decrease of the liquid refrigerant.
27. Superheat is the temperature increase of the vapor refrigerant.
28. Total Superheat is the temperature increase between where the refrigerant comes out of the saturated state as a vapor and where it enters the outdoor unit service port.
29. filter drier
30. liquid, vapor
31. absorbs
32. heat pump
33. refrigerant
34. reversing, metering devices
35. accumulator
36. T
37. F
38. F
39. F
40. F
41. T
42. T
43. T
44. three
45. four
46. five
47. two
48. one
49. five
50. two
51. three
52. one
53. four
54. piston
55. capillary tubing
56. TXV
57. a. 42˚ F, b. 55˚ F, c. 13˚ F
58. a. 36˚ F, b. 50˚ F, c. 14˚ F
59. a. 39˚ F, b. 54˚ F, c. 15˚ F
60. a. 95˚ F, b. 82˚ F, c. 13˚ F

Chapter 4:
1. F
2. T
3. F
4. F
5. T
6. saturated
7. Equalized
8. pressure, temperature
9. pounds per square inch
10. c
11. a
12. a
13. b
14. T
15. T
16. F
17. F
18. T
19. T
20. F
21. gauge, pump
22. same

Chapter 4 Continued:

23. different
24. air, water
25. analyzer
26. 2
27. 3
28. 1
29. F
30. T
31. F
32. T
33. T
34. T
35. f
36. d
37. e
38. c
39. b
40. a
41. Pounds per Square Inch Gauge
42. Pounds per Square Inch Absolute
43. 14.696 PSIA
44. 30" Hg
45. millimeters of Hg (or mm Hg)
46. 608
47. vapor
48. liquid
49. 15
50. c
51. a
52. d
53. c
54. d
55. F
56. T
57. T
58. F
59. T
60. blue gauge, blue hose, evaporator, large line, low side, suction, vapor
61. condenser, high side, liquid, red gauge, red hose, small line
62. c
63. b
64. b
65. b
66. d
67. a
68. b
69. saturated temperatures
70. superheat, subcooling
71. pressure
72. calibrated
73. bead, clamp
74. 50
75. 60
76. 110
77. 90
78. 40
79. 95
80. R-410A
81. a. 110
    b. 325
82. a. 44
    b. 98
83. a. 38
    b. 106
84. a. 40
    b. 110
85. R-410A
86. R-22

Chapter 4 Continued:

87. R-410A
88. R-22
89. recovery
90. charging

Chapter 5:

1. glasses, gloves
2. fresh air, SCBA
3. refrigerant gases
4. Protective Equipment
5. Self Contained, Apparatus
6. certification, refrigerant
7. www.epa.gov/section608
8. d
9. e
10. b
11. f
12. a
13. c
14. T
15. F
16. F
17. F
18. T
19. F
20. T
21. F
22. F
23. T
24. T
25. F
26. F
27. T
28. T
29. The purpose of the port cap is to keep the port connection clean and to seal in the refrigerant in the event there is a leak at the service valve or valve core.
30. The caps that do not have an o-ring are beveled on the inside in order to make a flare seal onto the port.
31. There are many companies making locking caps so technicians must have multiple brands of keys to unlock locking caps in order to service units.
32. Hoses with low loss fittings should be used to check the refrigerant charge to reduce accidental refrigerant loss due to connection and disconnection.

Chapter 6:

1. d
2. a
3. a
4. b
5. c
6. a
7. tubes
8. Front
9. Back
10. vacuum, recovery
11. Front, clockwise
12. Back
13. c
14. d
15. a
16. b
17. c
18. a
19. d

Chapter 6 Continued:

20. b
21. e
22. d
23. c
24. b
25. a
26. T
27. F
28. T
29. F
30. Two Position Service Valve
31. Three Position Service Valve
32. Back-Seat
33. Front-Seat
34. Mid-Seat
35. Front-Seat
36. Fully Open

Chapter 7:

1. T
2. F
3. T
4. F
5. T
6. manifold gauge
7. TXV
8. fixed orifice
9. pressures
10. saturated temperature
11. d
12. c
13. b
14. c
15. d
16. Subcooling is the temperature decrease of the liquid refrigerant as it rejects heat.
17. Comparing the actual and target subcooling verifies the charge level in the system.
18. The two most likely places to find subcooling on the outdoor unit are on the rating plate and on the back of the shroud.
19. It is important to get the actual subcooling as close as possible to the target subcooling to obtain an accurate refrigerant charge within the system.
20. Subcooling = Sat Temp − Actual Temp
21. TXV
22. high, liquid
23. Add
24. Recover
25. nothing, it's correct
26. 11
27. c
28. d
29. a
30. b
31. return, supply
32. superheat
33. total superheat, fixed orifice
34. actual, sat
35. one, 70°
36. F
37. T
38. T
39. F
40. T
41. b
42. d
43. b

44. a
45. c
46. before, return
47. outdoor unit
48. DB, WB
49. Add
50. Recover
51. e
52. c
53. b
54. f
55. d
56. a
57. F
58. T
59. T
60. F
61. T
62. F
63. T
64. 14
65. 9
66. [(3 x 66) – 80 – 90] / 2
    198 – 80 – 90 = 28 / 2 = 14°F
67. [(3 x 62) – 80 – 80] / 2
    186 – 80 – 80 = 26 / 2 = 13°F
68. The outside of the evaporator coil will start to attract humidity from the air in the building and freeze it (if the vapor saturated temp is below 32°F).
69. The indoor WB temp lowers as the system removes heat and humidity from the building. This change in WB temp will change the target superheat.
70. T
71. F
72. F
73. T
74. F
75. F
76. F
77. a
78. c
79. b
80. c
81. vacuum, exact amount
82. factory charge
83. electronic scale
84. rating plate
85. This unit is built with refrigerant sealed inside at the factory.
86. This is a conventional ducted system where the indoor coil and the outdoor coil are connected by the technician.
87. This is primarily a non-ducted system with one or more wall or ceiling mounted head units that are connected to the outdoor unit by the technician. However, ducted systems are available.
88. 50 – 15 = 35, 35 x .54 = 18.9oz,
    35 x .153 = 5.36oz,
    18.9 + 5.36 = 24.26oz
89. 25 – 10 = 15, 15 x .54 = 8.1oz,
    15 x .114 = 1.71oz,
    8.1 + 1.71 = 9.81oz
90. 55 – 25 = 30, 30 x .58 = 17.4oz,
    30 x .076 = 2.28oz,
    17.4 + 2.28 = 19.68oz
91. 12°F
92. 12°F

93. 15°F
94. a. 11°F
    b. 17°F
95. a. 9°F
    b. 10°F
96. a. 10°F
    b. 14°F
97. a. 15°F
    b. 11°F
98. a. 17°F
    b. 13°F
    c. correct charge
99. a. 21°F
    b. 11°F
    c. overcharged
100. a. 6°F
    b. 17°F
    c. overcharged
101. a. 10°F
    b. 5°F
    c. 14°F
    d. undercharged
102. a. 16°F
    b. 24°F
    c. 7°F
    d. undercharged
103. a. 20°F
    b. 6°F
    c. 22°F
    d. overcharged

Chapter 8:

1. F
2. F
3. F
4. F
5. T
6. purge air
7. open
8. off
9. compressor
10. higher
11. lower
12. higher
13. lower
14. c
15. b
16. a
17. d
18. Vapor
19. single
20. higher
21. low side vapor port
22. higher
23. T
24. F
25. F
26. T
27. running
28. adding, checking
29. add or charge (not both)
30. vapor
31. compressor, liquid
32. c
33. d
34. a
35. b
36. b
37. b
38. d

39. b
40. below
41. compressor
42. TXV
43. piston or capillary tubing
44. fixed orifice
45. lower
46. lower
47. target superheat
48. do
49. Recovery is the act of taking any amount of refrigerant out of the system and containing it in a recovery bottle.
50. A "full recovery" is when the full (entire) refrigerant charge is recovered and stored in a recovery bottle.
51. The term evacuation can refer to either vacuuming or to a full recovery.
52. Recovery can be done by either using the system's compressor while the system is running or by using a recovery machine while the system is off.
53. Care must be taken not to overfill a recovery bottle.
54. Bottle preparation is needed before using a new recovery bottle.
55. Do not mix multiple refrigerant types in a used recovery bottle.
56. Do not allow air or nitrogen to enter the recovery bottle.
57. Do not over-pressurize a recovery bottle.
58. d
59. f
60. b
61. e
62. c
63. a
64. T
65. F
66. T
67. F
68. F
69. T
70. T
71. T
72. F
73. short
74. air
75. charge
76. ports
77. locking, unauthorized
78. removed
79. a. 8°F
    b. 13°F
    c. 14°F
    d. overcharged
    e. recover
80. a. 8°F
    b. 14°F
    c. 10°F
    d. undercharged
    e. add
81. a. 9°F
    b. 2°F
    c. 18°F
    d. overcharged
    e. recover

Chapter 9:
1. F
2. T
3. T
4. F
5. F
6. nitrogen
7. 500
8. pump, gauge
9. standing vacuum test
10. neck
11. The bottle is free of moisture, noncondensables, and has no leaks.
12. electronic scale
13. This is done to avoid overfilling the bottle.
14. Tare Weight
15. Maximum Pressure Rating
16. Water Capacity
17. Maximum Temperature Rating
18. The last year the bottle was hydrostatically tested
19. c
20. a
21. b
22. d
23. c
24. c
25. 46 x .8 = 36.8lb
26. 28 x .8 = 22.4lb
27. 47 x .8 = 37.6,
    37.6 + 28 = 65.6,
    65.6lb
28. 48 x .8 = 38.4,
    38.4 + 25 = 63.4,
    63.4 - 55 = 8.4
    8.4lb
29. T
30. T
31. F
32. F
33. T
34. T
35. not to
36. not to
37. liquid
38. similar to
39. refrigerant analyzer
40. connection, leak
41. purged
42. vacuumed
43. identification tag
44. empty vacuumed
45. d
46. a
47. a
48. d
49. b
50. d
51. d
52. a
53. c
54. T
55. T
56. T
57. F
58. F
59. Monitor the vacuum level at the gauge or display for ten minutes to see if it rises.
60. An increase in pressure indicates that left over liquid refrigerant has phase

Chapter 9 Continued:
changed into a vapor and applied pressure inside the system.
61. The recovery bottle valve can be closed and the hoses can be disconnected.
62. The recovery machine needs to be turned on again.
63. If this occurs, turn the flow valve on the recovery machine to the purge function. Turn the recovery machine back on until the internal pressure is below the required vacuum level and then turn the machine off.
64. contaminated
65. correct refrigerant
66. 48 x .8 = 38.4
    38.4 + 28 = 66.4
    66.4 - 49 = 17.4
    17.4
67. 47 x .8 = 37.6
    37.6 + 27 = 64.6
    64.6 - 35 = 29.6
    29.6
68. 26 x .8 = 20.8
    20.8 + 15 = 35.8
    35.8 - 19 = 16.8
    16.8

Chapter 10:
1. 2
2. 5
3. 4
4. 1
5. 3
6. 7
7. 6
8. line set
9. vapor, liquid
10. vapor
11. ream, clean
12. brazed, soldered
13. F
14. T
15. T
16. F
17. b
18. c
19. d
20. d
21. c
22. c
23. nitrogen
24. metering device
25. lubrication
26. pressure test
27. an equal
28. TXVs
29. indoor
30. lowers
31. lower
32. A decrease in pressure during a pressure test most likely indicates a leak in the system.
33. A longer pressure test should be performed if a small leak in the system is suspected.
34. A leak may develop if a new system is pressure tested to a higher pressure than the stated max design pressure.
35. Because they are more susceptible to developing leaks, older systems should be

Chapter 10 Continued:
pressure tested at a lower pressure than newer systems.
36. T
37. F
38. T
39. F
40. T
41. T
42. bubble, ultrasonic, electronic, fluorescent
43. pump down, recover
44. 0, air
45. oil blowout
46. vacuum procedure
47. moisture, air, nitrogen
48. d
49. d
50. b
51. d
52. b
53. d
54. a
55. e
56. c
57. rises
58. metering device
59. removal
60. vacuum
61. close to
62. off
63. gas ballast
64. reinstall
65. lower
66. 200-300
67. attached to
68. valved off from
69. ten
70. T
71. F
72. F
73. F
74. T
75. T
76. T
77. oil, off
78. pressure, off
79. pressure test, oil blowout
80. removal tools
81. valve cores
82. oil
83. manufacturer's
84. c
85. d
86. c
87. b
88. d
89. open
90. bottle
91. does not
92. prior to
93. filter drier
94. d
95. e
96. c
97. a
98. b
99. F
100. F
101. F
102. T

Chapter 10 Continued:
103. T
104. T
105. T
106. Slightly restrict the vacuum hose set-up to slow the vacuum process.
107. Add heat to the system by running the indoor fan.
108. If a gas furnace is part of the split system, the heat can be turned on.
109. A crankcase heater (at the compressor) or heat blankets (on the tubing or coils) can be used.
110. Perform a triple evacuation instead of a single evacuation.
111. If the micron level does not rise during a standing vacuum test, this indicates that a single evacuation has been successful.
112. A triple evacuation includes breaking the vacuum with nitrogen twice and vacuuming three times in order to remove water vapor from the system.
113. Run the vacuum to a level of 1000 microns, break the vacuum with nitrogen, vacuum again to 600 microns, break the vacuum with nitrogen, vacuum to a level of 300 microns and perform the standing vacuum test.
114. The purpose of flowing nitrogen for 5 minutes prior to running the vacuum pump again is to purge water vapor from the system.
115. As water vapor is pulled out of the system, it gets stuck in vacuum oil. This oil must be replaced with new oil in order to produce a deep vacuum.
116. The vacuum oil may need to be changed while vacuuming a system with a high water level.

Chapter 11:
1. F
2. T
3. T
4. F
5. T
6. 4
7. 1
8. 3
9. 2
10. The leak point will allow air to be pulled into the system while in vacuum.
11. This could cause the coil to burst due to the limited volume to store refrigerant.
12. It could damage the compressor due to an electrical arc from the motor windings to the ground frame.
13. The running fan will introduce a steady source of heat at the indoor coil for the refrigerant to absorb. This will help vaporize the liquid refrigerant.
14. The remaining refrigerant must be recovered down to the required vacuum level.
15. b
16. c
17. a
18. d
19. internal
20. only needs to be partially

Chapter 11 Continued:
21. internal pressure relief valve is
22. compressor valves are
23. compressor
24. indoor

Chapter 12:
1. T
2. F
3. T
4. T
5. T
6. d
7. a
8. b
9. a
10. d
11. d
12. b
13. +30
14. +25
15. sweating
16. cold, vapor
17. Delta
18. pressure, temperature
19. saturated, low
20. diagnosis
21. Delta T
22. overcharge
23. charge
24. heat transfer
25. added
26. low
27. does not
28. T
29. T
30. F
31. T
32. T
33. F
34. d
35. c
36. b
37. a
38. They cannot verify that the refrigerant is completely in the vapor state before the refrigerant enters. If the saturated refrigerant enters, it can lead to compressor failure.
39. The return air temp is measured a few feet before the indoor coil and the supply air temp is measured a few feet after the coil. Delta T = Return Temp – Supply Temp
40. Examples include when the system is overcharged, has low airflow, or has a low side sat temp below 32 ˚F.
41. This occurs when there is a high WB temperature in the building and a high DB temperature outside, especially on systems that have a fixed orifice metering device.
42. depending on
43. fixed orifice
44. TXV
45. TXV

Chapter 13:
1. T
2. T
3. F
4. T

Chapter 13 Continued:
5. F
6. T
7. T
8. frozen
9. compressor
10. three, water vapor
11. below, normal, high
12. below, low, low
13. normal, low
14. high, low
15. undersized ducts, collapsed ducts, undersized or blocked grilles and/or registers, clogged air filter, dust clogging the indoor coil, dust clogging the secondary heat exchanger of a furnace, low blower speed, dirty blower wheel, broken blower motor, static pressure is too high.
16. hunting
17. a leak
18. high, high
19. strainer
20. closed
21. F
22. T
23. T
24. F
25. F
26. F
27. F
28. T
29. T
30. T
31. T
32. d
33. b
34. c
35. a
36. leaking compressor valves
37. reversing valve
38. High, High
39. less
40. T
41. F
42. T
43. T
44. T
45. F
46. d
47. b
48. a
49. e
50. c
51. The problem is Low Indoor airflow.
52. The problem is a Liquid Line Restriction.
53. a. 23˚F
    b. 67˚F
    c. 44˚F
    d. 78˚F
    e. 77˚F
    f. 1˚F
    g. Low Refrigerant Charge
54. a. 30˚F
    b. 31˚F
    c. 1˚F
    d. 101˚F
    e. 90˚F
    f. 11˚F
    g. Low Indoor Airflow
55. a. 29˚F

Chapter 13 Continued:
55. b. 68°F
    c. 39°F
    d. 82°F
    e. 80°F
    f. 2°F
    g. Low Refrigerant Charge
56. a. 26°F
    b. 70°F
    c. 44°F
    d. 108°F
    e. 90°F
    f. 18°F
    g. Liquid Line Restriction
57. a. 39°F
    b. 52°F
    c. 13°F
    d. 117°F
    e. 92°F
    f. 25°F
    g. Overcharged
58. a. 52°F
    b. 54°F
    c. 2°F
    d. 105°F
    e. 100°F
    f. 5°F
    g. Uninsulated, Detached TXV Bulb
59. a. 62°F
    b. 75°F
    c. 13°F
    d. 78°F
    e. 68°F
    f. 10°F
    g. Weak Compressor or Reversing Valve
       Bleeding Across the Tubes
60. a. 49°F
    b. 50°F
    c. 1°F
    d. 115°F
    e. 91°F
    f. 24°F
    g. Overcharged

Chapter 14:
1. T
2. F
3. T
4. T
5. F
6. F
7. T
8. d
9. d
10. c
11. d
12. No, an R-22 TXV cannot be used in an R-410A system. The system will likely hunt and have a high superheat.
13. Yes, an R-22 TXV can be used in an R-407C system because these two refrigerants have similar boiling points.
14. A TXV will increase efficiency, better protect the compressor, and allows for sub-cooling to be used to check the charge.
15. A poor installation or poor service procedure can allow water to mix with the oil in a system.
16. The chemical result of water and refrigerant oil mixing together is acid and alcohol. They eat away at the internal

Chapter 14 Continued:
components within a system.
17. an oil treatment
18. test kit
19. oil bubbling
20. compressor
21. undersized
22. oversized

Chapter 15:
1. Cubic Feet per Minute
2. BTU / HR
3. indoor coil, compressor
4. 12,000, 400
5. 3, 36,000
6. 350
7. c
8. a
9. b
10. d
11. F
12. T
13. F
14. T
15. F
16. F
17. T
18. T
19. T
20. f
21. b
22. d
23. a
24. e
25. c
26. h
27. g
28. 400
29. supply
30. return
31. Static pressure
32. abnormally high
33. manufacturer's
34. (241 x 21 x 3.414) / (1.08 x 20)
    17,278 / 21.6
    799.91
35. 0.47
36. clogged, 0.25

Chapter 16:
1. T
2. F
3. T
4. F
5. T
6. a. nut
   b. teflon ring
   c. piston chamber
   d. piston chamber end
   e. piston
   f. distributor tubes
7. a. bulb
   b. power head
   c. external equalizer
   d. diaphragm
   e. inlet tube
   f. outlet tube
   g. push rod
   h. pin
   i. spring
   j. pin carrier

Chapter 16 Continued:
8. a. P1
   b. P2
   c. P3
9. c
10. a
11. c
12. a
13. c
14. distributor
15. superheat
16. superheat
17. compressor, saturated
18. Thermostatic Expansion Valve
19. orifice
20. b
21. e
22. d
23. a
24. c
25. internal, inactive
26. adjustable
27. stem
28. decreases
29. increases
30. nonadjustable
31. capillary
32. vapor
33. T
34. F
35. F
36. T
37. F
38. F
39. T
40. c
41. c
42. b
43. a
44. c
45. b
46. upward
47. vapor
48. vapor, 2, 10
49. fixed
50. Electronic Expansion Valve
51. Automatic Expansion Valve
52. strainer, filter drier
53. closed
54. superheat, subcooling
55. solenoid
56. c
57. e
58. b
59. d
60. a

Chapter 17:
1. T
2. F
3. T
4. F
5. T
6. F
7. T
8. b
9. c
10. a
11. factory
12. mineral oil, POE
13. miscibility

14. b
15. c
16. a
17. c
18. a
19. a. Mineral Oil
    b. Polyolester Oil
    c. Alkylbenzene Oil
    d. Polyalkylene Glycol Oil
20. Miscibility is the ability of the refrigerant and the refrigerant oil to mix together in order for the oil to be carried through the system by the refrigerant.
21. The oil type and total oil weight can be found on the rating plate.
22. R-22
23. R-410A
24. When water mixes with refrigerant oil, it creates alcohol and/or acids. This wears down seals inside the system and the resin insulation covering the electrical windings of the compressor.
25. less
26. combines with
27. carbon
28. line set
29. raining
30. T
31. F
32. T
33. T
34. F
35. T
36. b
37. e
38. d
39. a
40. c
41. c
42. d
43. a
44. b
45. pressure test, vacuum
46. 50', mini-split
47. Air Conditioning Refrigeration
48. vapor, liquid
49. mini-split
50. 3/8"
51. 5/8"
52. 60,000
53. Hermetic, pump
54. vapor, liquid
55. a. 50 - 25 = 25', 25 x .58 = 14.5,
       25 x .1 = 2.5, 14.5 + 2.5 = 17
    b. 14.5oz
    c. 2.5oz
    d. 17oz
56. a. 40 - 15 = 25, 25 x .54 = 13.5,
       25 x .114 = 2.85
    b. 13.5oz
    c. 2.85oz
    d. 16.08oz
57. The evaporator is located immediately after the metering device and is where the refrigerant changes from a low pressure, low temperature liquid, to a saturated state, and then to a superheated vapor.
58. The condenser is located immediately after the compressor and is where the refrigerant changes from a superheated

vapor, to a saturated state, and then to a completely subcooled liquid.
59. The coils change their function when the refrigerant flow reverses.
60. The accumulator is a protection device for the compressor as well as a storage tank for the refrigerant. It is located on the suction line directly before the compressor.
61. There is a metering device near the bottom of the tank that allows the oil and liquid refrigerant to be metered into the suction line a little at a time.
62. T
63. F
64. F
65. T
66. a
67. c
68. d
69. b
70. heat pump
71. receiver
72. receiver, pump down
73. king valve
74. front
75. e
76. f
77. d
78. c
79. b
80. a
81. a. rotary
    b. scroll
    c. reciprocating
82. a. rotary
    b. reciprocating
    c. scroll
83. a. discharge line
    b. pilot valve
    c. electrical solenoid
    d. pilot valve tubing
    e. suction line

Appendix A:

1. T
2. T
3. F
4. F
5. F
6. T

Appendix B:

1. Heat loss is the amount of heat lost hourly from the building during low outdoor temperatures.
2. Heat gain is the amount of heat gained hourly in the building due to people, appliances, and/or outdoor temperatures.
3. The reasons are to guarantee system efficiency, to make sure the system can handle the heat load and loss of the building, to help the lifespan of the system, to keep noise levels reasonable, to properly reduce humidity levels, and to show that care and consideration are taken when sizing a system.
4. d
5. a
6. b

7. F
8. F
9. T
10. F
11. T
12. F
13. · commercial or residential use
    · maximum occupancy
    · zip code
    · design temperatures
    · volume of the building
    · gross exterior walls
    · inside finishing and outside sheathing, insulation R-value
    · exterior door and window sizes and U-value, orientation, leakage, glass type and frame type
    · skylight U-value, orientation, glass type and frame type
    · floor dimensions, type of flooring insulation value underneath, and if there is any ventilation underneath
    · ceiling dimensions, ceiling type, rafter height, insulation value, ventilation above, encapsulation, and if the ceiling is a cathedral
    · lighting specifications for heat offset
    · appliances for heat offset
    · tightness of the building
    · room sizes and percentage of the load or loss
    · location of the duct, whether inside or outside the structure, or in the attic or crawlspace, as well as insulation value, and leakage
    · mechanical ventilation, if used

Appendix C:

1. two or more
2. pressure, glide
3. a different
4. dew, bubble
5. bubble
6. dew
7. c
8. a
9. b
10. a
11. a
12. Fractionation is the potential for a single component refrigerant within a blend refrigerant to leak out faster than the other single component refrigerants.
13. The severity of the change depends on whether the unit is mainly running or mainly off during the leakage. If the unit is mainly running while leaking, the system will leak each single component refrigerant at a more even rate.
14. The refrigerant will exit the bottle at the correct composition only while in the liquid state.
15. Saturated Bubble Temp – Actual Temp on Liquid Line
16. Actual Temp on Vapor Line – Saturated Dew Temp

Circle the best answer for each statement/question.

45. Which component or tool can be used to recover refrigerant while a system is off?

    a. compressor

    b. condenser

    c. manifold gauge set

    d. self-contained recovery machine

46. A self-contained recovery machine can recover refrigerant without the assistance of a system's...

    a. compressor.

    b. condenser.

    c. manifold gauge set.

    d. TXV.

47. When a recovery machine is used, which component should be mounted to the inlet of the machine in order to keep both it and the recovery bottle clean?

    a. filter drier

    b. TXV

    c. evaporator

    d. valve cores

48. Which component should be removed before recovery so that the port openings on the system are not restricted?

    a. filter drier

    b. TXV

    c. evaporator

    d. valve cores

49. Which component(s) should be used to speed up the recovery time?

    a. hoses with valve core depressors

    b. short, larger diameter hoses without valve core depressors

    c. long, smaller diameter hoses without valve core depressors

    d. an automatic low loss valve

50. Which tool is used to take the valve core out of the port prior to recovering the refrigerant?

    a. three-position service valve

    b. valve core depressor

    c. valve core torque wrench

    d. valve core removal tool

51. Which of these occurs as a result of the valve cores being removed prior to recovery?

    a. a more accurate pressure reading during recovery

    b. a reduction in the amount of time it takes to recover the refrigerant from the system

    c. the possibility of the pressure rising after the recovery machine is turned off is reduced

    d. All of the above

52. What occurs if the valve cores are left in the service ports during recovery?

    a. the refrigerant flow will be restricted

    b. the recovery will be performed too quickly

    c. the valve cores may be damaged

    d. All of the above

53. Prior to recovery, the air should be purged from the refrigerant hoses at the recovery bottle port connection while the recovery bottle valve is in which position?

    a. fully open

    b. half open

    c. fully closed/off

    d. All these positions are acceptable

Circle T for True and F for False.

54. **T / F** It's helpful to have the system's indoor blower fan running while performing the recovery process.

55. **T / F** Both the outlet pressure and inlet pressure on the recovery machine need to be monitored while the recovery machine is on.

56. **T / F** The outlet pressure on the recovery machine should not exceed the maximum pressure rating listed on the recovery bottle.

57. **T / F** If the outlet pressure on the recovery machine reaches the maximum pressure, keep the recovery machine running until the pressure reduces.

58. **T / F** 4" HG = 0 PSIG

Answer the following with complete sentences.

59. After the recovery reaches the required vacuum level and the recovery machine is turned off, what needs to be monitored and for how long? _____
_____

60. What does an increase in pressure indicate has happened? _____
_____
_____

61. If the vacuum level remains steady while the recovery machine is off, what can be done? _____
_____
_____

62. If the vacuum level rises above the required vacuum level, what needs to be done? _____
_____

63. For a recovery machine with a purge function, what can be done after the vacuum level in the system remains steady while the recovery machine is off? _____
_____
_____
_____

Use each image to solve the following questions.

64. Is this R-410A recovery bottle contaminated or does it have the correct refrigerant? Circle <u>contaminated</u> or <u>correct refrigerant</u>.

65. Is this R-410A recovery bottle contaminated or does it have the correct refrigerant? Circle <u>contaminated</u> or <u>correct refrigerant</u>.

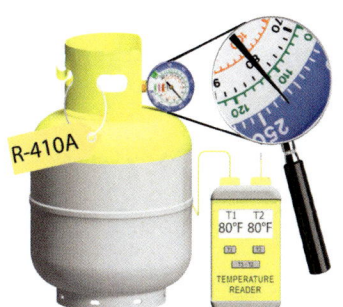

66. Determine the remaining refrigerant capacity inside this 50 lb recovery bottle. This bottle has a TW of 28 lb, a WC of 48 lb, and can only be filled to 80% capacity.

_____ lb

67. Determine the remaining refrigerant capacity inside this 50 lb recovery bottle. This bottle has a TW of 27 lb, a WC of 47 lb, and can only be filled to 80% capacity.

_____ lb

68. Determine the remaining refrigerant capacity inside this 30 lb recovery bottle. This bottle has a TW of 15 lb, a WC of 26 lb, and can only be filled to 80% capacity.

_____ lb

CHAPTER 10

System Preparation Prior to Adding Refrigerant

When installing a split type air conditioning system, there is a multi-step process that must be performed to prepare the refrigerant tubing prior to adding refrigerant.

Number the following steps for "preparing the refrigerant tubing prior to adding refrigerant" in order from Step 1-7.

1. Step # _____ : Pressure test the system.

2. Step # _____ : Perform the vacuum procedure.

3. Step # _____ : Perform the oil blow out procedure when working on an existing system.

4. Step # _____ : Install the refrigerant vapor and liquid tubes from the indoor unit to the outdoor unit.

5. Step # _____ : Perform a leak detection on the system.

6. Step # _____ : Break the vacuum with refrigerant from the system or from the bottle.

7. Step # _____ : Verify the vacuum level with the standing vacuum test.

Fill in the blanks with the correct word(s).

8. The tubing is referred to as _____ _____ .

9. The tubing consists of a _____ line and a _____ line.

10. The _____ line is the larger of the two tubes.

11. Cut, _____ and _____ the line set tubing ends before connecting

    them to the indoor and outdoor units.

12. Line set connections are typically _____ or _____ in place.

Circle T for True or F for False.

13. **T / F** By code, the line set can only run through the crawlspace or attic of a building.

14. **T / F** Line set connections to the indoor and outdoor units are sometimes crimped or flared, or use a

    factory supplied connection.

15. **T / F** If a filter drier is not already installed inside the outdoor unit, one must be installed in the liquid

    line upstream from the metering device.

16. **T / F** It is best to install the filter drier outside the building rather than inside it.

Circle the best answer for each statement/question.

17. Manufacturers of residential mini-split systems usually…

    a. recommend adding a filter drier to a new system.

    b. do not recommend adding a filter drier to a new system.

    c. recommend adding a TXV to the indoor unit.

    d. recommend adding multiple filter driers to a new system.

18. In order to prevent the creation of oxidation in the tubing during high temp brazing,…

    a. cool the outside of the tubing prior to and during brazing.

    b. be sure to braze in a location that is at least 70° F.

    c. add a small volumetric flow of inert gas through the tubing prior to and during brazing.

    d. All of the above

19. Brazing is typically performed using…

    a. an air-acetylene torch setup.   b. an oxy-acetylene torch setup.

    c. Neither a nor b   d. Both a and b

20. Silver bearing braze rods have a melting point of approximately…

    a. 100° F.   b. 212° F.   c. 1,000° F.   d. 1350° F.

21. Which of these gases is the most commonly used one for air purging?

    a. Ammonia   b. Hydrogen   c. Nitrogen   d. Oxygen

22. In order to control the flow of the gas used in air purging, install a regulator to the tank and attach this device to the regulator.

    a. pressure gauge   b. on/off valve   c. flow meter   d. refrigerant analyzer

Circle the correct bold term(s).

23. To flow **nitrogen / oxygen** through an empty system, the valves cores at the ports must be removed.

24. Oxidation flakes can clog the strainer, filter drier and/or the **compressor / metering device.**

25. Oxidation in the tubing can lead to a lack of **lubrication / pressure** at the compressor.

26. Once the refrigerant line set is connected to the system, a **pressure test / vacuum procedure** must be performed to verify that leaks do not exist.

27. Adding nitrogen through both service ports may help to maintain **a higher / an equal** pressure on both sides of the system.

Circle the correct bold term(s).

28. Some **TXVs / pistons** do not allow full equalization of the nitrogen pressure test.

29. A split system's max test pressure can be found on the rating plate of the **indoor / outdoor** unit.

30. After adding nitrogen into a system to pressure test it, wait at least 10 minutes to see if the pressure **lowers / rises**.

31. A pressure test on a new system can be performed using a pressure slightly **lower / higher** than the max design pressure.

Answer the following with complete sentences.

32. During a pressure test, what does a decrease in pressure in a system most likely indicate? _____

_____

33. Why would a longer pressure test such as for 24 hours be performed? _____

_____

34. Why must a new system *not* be pressure tested to a higher pressure than the max design pressure

listed at the indoor coil? _____

_____

_____

35. Why should older systems be pressure tested at a lower pressure than newer systems? _____

_____

_____

_____

Circle T for True or F for False.

36. **T / F** When a system is found to be low on refrigerant during a service call, leak detection should be performed.

37. **T / F** Low superheat indicates a low refrigerant charge which may have been caused by a leak in the system.

38. **T / F** Non-corrosive bubble leak detector covering over a leak spot will usually produce bubbles or a foaming action.

39. **T / F** Non-corrosive bubble leak detector is the only detector needed for finding all leaks.

40. **T / F** If a leak is suspected on an empty system, one ounce of refrigerant can be added to the system along with a nitrogen pressure test to search for leaks with an electronic sniffing tool.

41. **T / F** A nitrogen pressure test including one ounce of refrigerant can be released into the atmosphere per EPA 608 guidelines.

Fill in the blanks with the correct word(s).

42. There are a variety of refrigerant leak detection tools such as non corrosive _____ leak detector, _____ leak detector, _____ sniffing tool, and _____ dye.

43. After finding a leak on a system with refrigerant inside, either _____ _____ or _____ the refrigerant.

44. Do not draw the system down below _____ "Hg or _____ will enter the tubing through the leak spot.

45. An _____ _____ procedure is performed on an existing empty system prior to performing the vacuum in order to blow the oil onto the inner walls of the tubing.

46. Pushing the refrigerant oil onto the inner walls of the tubing ensures that sections of the tubing are not blocked during the _____ _____.

47. A vacuum procedure is performed in order to remove any _____ , _____ , and/or _____ from the system prior to adding refrigerant.

Circle the best answer for each statement/question.

48. A vacuum pump is used to...

    a. increase pressure inside the system in order to boil any water in the tubing.

    b. decrease pressure inside the system in order to boil any water in the tubing.

    c. remove water, nitrogen, and/or air from the system.

    d. Only b and c

49. The vacuum procedure is also known as...

    a. recovery.　　　b. evacuation.　　　c. dehydration.　　　d. Only b and c

50. The electrical windings in a hermetic or semi-hermetic compressor are coated with resin insulation. If acid breaks down the resin insulation...

    a. the system will not remove heat from the building as effectively.

    b. the electrical wires will touch each other causing the compressor to burn out.

    c. new resin can be added to the compressor through the system ports.

    d. Only b and c

51. Any water left in the system will mix with the refrigerant oil, which may create...

    a. toxic fumes.　　　b. alcohol.　　　c. acids.　　　d. Only b and c

Match the left hand column items with those in the right hand column.

52. _____ The vacuum level cannot be accurately...

53. _____ A contaminated refrigerant charge will run at high operating pressures...

54. _____ The target vacuum level for a system during the vacuum procedure is...

55. _____ The vacuum gauge must be...

56. _____ When the vacuum pump is off and isolated...

a. 500 microns or lower.

b. measured by reading the inch Hg level on the compound gauge.

c. the standing vacuum test measures the true vacuum level in the system.

d. and not effectively absorb and reject heat while the system runs.

e. monitored during both the vacuum procedure and the standing vacuum test.

Circle the correct bold term(s).

57. After reaching a vacuum below 500 microns, isolate the vacuum pump from the system in order to perform a "standing vacuum test" for 10 minutes to see if the micron level **rises / falls**.

58. When possible, do not pull a vacuum from only one side of the system because the **evaporator coil / metering device** in the middle of the system's tubing acts like a restriction.

59. Connect a valve core **depressor / removal** tool for the valve core at each port prior to and during the vacuum procedure.

60. Use a **vacuum / pressure** rated ball valve in order to isolate the vacuum gauge from the system prior to breaking the vacuum with refrigerant.

61. For an accurate vacuum measurement, keep the vacuum gauge **close to / away from** the system's service ports and away from the pump.

62. While performing the vacuum procedure, the compressor's electrical power must remain **on / off.**

63. The use of a **valve core removal tool / gas ballast** helps prevent any initial air or other gas in the system from contaminating the vacuum pump oil.

64. Use valve core removal tools to **reinstall / remove** the valve cores after breaking the vacuum with refrigerant and after there is positive refrigerant pressure in the system.

65. The system must be vacuumed to a level of 500 microns or **higher / lower.**

66. A good target micron level is **200-300 / 500-600** microns.

67. Perform the standing vacuum test while the vacuum gauge is **attached to / detached from** the system.

68. Perform the standing vacuum test while the vacuum pump and hoses are **connected to / valved off from** the system.

69. Perform the standing vacuum test for at least **five / ten** minutes to see if the system's vacuum level rises.

Circle T for True or F for False.

70. **T / F** The vacuum level read during the standing vacuum test is the true vacuum level.

71. **T / F** The vacuum level read when the vacuum pump is running is the true vacuum level.

72. **T / F** To get a more accurate reading while the vacuum pump is running, it is best to keep the vacuum gauge as far from the system ports as possible.

73. **T / F** If the vacuum level does not rise above 1000 microns during the standing vacuum test, the system is ready for refrigerant to be added.

74. **T / F** During the standing vacuum test, the micron level will rise to a level that is too high for the vacuum gauge to read if there is a leak in the system.

75. **T / F** During the standing vacuum test, the micron level will rise, stop for a bit, rise again, and then stop again when there is water in the system.

76. **T / F** The correct procedure after a successful standing vacuum test is to valve off the vacuum gauge prior to adding refrigerant into the system.

Fill in the blanks with the correct word(s).

77. When breaking the vacuum, the vacuum gauge sensor can be contaminated by _____ that is mixed with the refrigerant unless the vacuum gauge is first valved _____.

78. The addition of refrigerant into the system creates high _____ which may damage the vacuum gauge unless the vacuum gauge has been valved _____.

79. Two procedures that are performed prior to the vacuum procedure are the _____ _____ and the _____ _____.

80. To connect the vacuum setup, attach valve core _____ _____ to the two service valve ports on the outdoor unit.

81. Remove the _____ _____ from the ports of the empty system before vacuuming.

82. When breaking the vacuum with refrigerant from the system, the order in which the service valves are opened affects the location of the _____ during the initial start up.

83. When breaking the vacuum with refrigerant from the system, follow the _____ instructions for which service valve to open first.

Circle the best answer for each statement/question.

84. If unsure which valve to open first (liquid or vapor), before opening the valves, break the vacuum with...

    a. nitrogen.   b. air.

    c. a small amount of refrigerant from the bottle.   d. None of the above

85. To break the vacuum with refrigerant from the system, open the vapor and liquid line service valves by turning each valve stem...

    a. clockwise from the back-seat position.

    b. counterclockwise from the back-seat position.

    c. clockwise from the front-seat position.

    d. counterclockwise from the front-seat position.

86. After refrigerant is introduced to break the vacuum, the refrigerant inside the tubing causes the entire system to be at..

    a. the max design pressure.   b. negative pressure. c. positive pressure.   d. None of the above

87. After breaking the vacuum with refrigerant, make sure to first...

    a. remove the valve cores.   b. reinstall the valve cores.

    c. remove the valve core removal tools.   d. attach hoses and the manifold set.

88. To break the vacuum with refrigerant from an outdoor unit's three position service valves, use a...

    a. a valve core removal tool.   b. valve core depressor.

    c. a vacuum gauge.   d. a ratcheting service wrench.

Circle the correct bold term(s).

89. A dry empty system must be vacuumed while the service valves are in the **open / closed** position.

90. To compensate for an extra long line set attached to the system, break the vacuum with refrigerant from the **system / bottle**.

91. A dry unit is a new outdoor unit that **does / does not** come with refrigerant inside.

92. In the case of a leak in the system, it should be found and fixed **after / prior to** vacuuming.

93. A new **filter drier / accumulator** must be installed any time the system is open for service and before doing the final pressure test, oil blowout, and vacuum.

Match the left hand column items with those in the right hand column.

94. _____ The small size of the hex key adapter...   a. is used to hold the service valve still while turning the stem.

95. _____ The large size of the hex key adapter...   b. are used on two position service valves.

96. _____ The ratcheting service wrench...   c. is used on three position service valves without a hex key adapter.

97. _____ An adjustable wrench or open-end wrench...

98. _____ The ratcheting service wrench and hex key adapter...   d. is used on the liquid line service valve stem.

    e. is used for the vapor line service valve stem.

Circle T for True or F for False.

99. **T / F** In order to weigh in many pounds of refrigerant while the system is off, break the vacuum with vapor refrigerant from the bottle.

100. **T / F** An empty packaged unit that has a factory charge of 10 lb can be fully charged by turning on the compressor and quickly weighing in the total amount of liquid refrigerant into the system.

101. **T / F** If the pressure in the bottle and the system are the same, put the bottle in ice water to continue adding refrigerant into the system.

102. **T / F** A small amount of refrigerant can be added to the system via the low pressure side of a running system.

103. **T / F** A warming blanket can be used to warm up a refrigerant bottle in order to increase the pressure inside the bottle.

104. **T / F** If the micron level rises during the standing vacuum test there is either water vapor or a leak in the system.

105. **T /F** A fast vacuum can be accomplished as long as the tubing or coils have a way to absorb heat.

Answer the following with complete sentences.

To reduce the chance of water freezing inside the tubing during a vacuum, <u>one</u> or <u>more</u> of the following methods can be used:

106. Method 1: _____

_____

107. Method 2: _____

_____

108. Method 3: _____

_____

109. Method 4: _____

_____

110. Method 5: _____

_____

Answer the following with complete sentences.

111. During a standing vacuum test, what evidence shows that a single evacuation has been successful?

_____

_____

112. What is a triple evacuation?

_____

_____

_____

113. Give an example of the steps to perform a triple evacuation?

_____

_____

_____

_____

114. After breaking the vacuum with nitrogen during a triple evacuation, what is the purpose of flowing nitrogen for 5 minutes before running the vacuum pump again?

_____

_____

_____

115. Why must the vacuum pump oil be changed regularly?

_____

_____

_____

116. Give an example of when the vacuum oil may need to be changed out **during** the middle of the vacuum process in order to finish the process.

_____

_____

_____

CHAPTER 11
The Pump Down Procedure

Circle T for True or F for False.

1. **T / F** The pump down of a split system is performed by using the system's compressor to pump all the refrigerant from the outdoor unit into the indoor unit.

2. **T / F** During the pump down of a split system, the refrigerant is locked and stored in the outdoor unit.

3. **T / F** The pump down procedure is usually performed prior to replacing the indoor coil, metering device, filter drier, or line set.

4. **T / F** After the outdoor unit of a split system is relocated, a pump down should be performed.

5. **T / F** Some manufacturers may recommend not to perform the pump down procedure on a system with a scroll compressor.

List the following steps to the Pump Down Procedure in order from Step (1-4).

6.   Step # _____: Monitor the vacuum level while the system is off to make sure that it does not rise above the required vacuum level.

7.   Step # _____: Front-Seat the liquid line service valve while the system is running.

8.   Step # _____: After both service valves are shut, immediately turn off the compressor.

9.   Step # _____: Once the compressor moves all the refrigerant into the outdoor unit, front seat the vapor service valve.

Answer the following with complete sentences.

10. Why must a system that has a leak not be pumped down to a level below 0" Hg?

_____

_____

11. Why must a pump down procedure *not* be performed on a system with a Micro-channel condenser coil? _____

_____

12. Why must a pump down procedure *not* be performed to a level below 5 PSIG on a scroll compressor?

_____

_____

13. During a pump down procedure, why should the indoor fan be running?

_____

_____

_____

14. The objective is to perform a successful pump down with a final vacuum level that does not

rise. If the vacuum level rises what must be done? _____

_____

_____

Match the left hand column items with those in the right hand column.

15. _____ Pump down the system to a slightly lower

vacuum level than what is required so that when...

16. _____ Keep a heat source running...

17. _____ Add heat to the refrigerant in order to...

18. _____ Always install a new filter drier after

any work is completed and prior to the...

a. vaporize any liquid refrigerant.

b. the compressor is off, the vacuum level

   does not rise above the required level.

c. at the evaporator coil while the pump

   down is being performed.

d. pressure test and vacuum.

Circle the correct bold term(s).

19. The pump down procedure can be used to troubleshoot whether the compressor has weak valves or a weak **external / internal** pressure relief valve.

20. The system **needs to be fully / only needs to be partially** pumped down in order to see if the compressor is strong enough.

21. If the compressor starts to pump down and then makes a squealing noise followed by an increase in vapor pressure, this indicates that the **compressor valves are / internal pressure relief valve is** weak.

22. When performing the pump down procedure, if the refrigerant pressures lower a bit but then stay at the same pressure, this indicates that the **compressor valves are / internal pressure relief valve is** likely the problem.

23. If the system's refrigerant is able to be pumped down, the **condenser / compressor** is not the problem.

24. If the vapor pressure is abnormally high while the system is running in air conditioning mode, look for an excessively high heat load on the **indoor / outdoor** coil and investigate the reversing valve (if equipped), because one of these may be the problem.

CHAPTER 12
Other Charging Methods

Circle T for True or F for False.

1. **T / F** There is a third service port with a valve core on most single or two speed split system heat pumps.

2. **T / F** The third service port on a single or two speed split system heat pump is connected to the liquid tube right at the inlet to the compressor.

3. **T / F** The third service port on a single or two speed split system heat pump can be referred to as the true suction port.

4. **T / F** The low side pressure can be read at this third port whether the split system is in heating or cooling mode.

5. **T / F** When connecting the manifold gauge set to a heat pump in cooling mode to add refrigerant from the bottle, make sure to connect the blue low side hose to the large vapor service valve port.

Circle the best answer for each statement/question.

6. What are some negative factors to consider when restricting the outdoor airflow during a pre-summer preventative maintenance to check the charge?
    a. the lower accuracy of this charging method
    b. the time it takes to set up the airflow restriction
    c. the likelihood that the indoor temp will not be above 70° F
    d. All of the above

7. Restricting the condenser fan airflow to check the refrigerant charge of a system when the outdoor temp is low, can only be done on a system running in cooling mode, when the indoor temp is 70° F or above, and on a system that uses what type of metering device?
    a. TXV   b. piston   c. capillary tubing   d. All of the above

8. When is it suggested to check the refrigerant charge of a system operating in heating mode, using the superheat or subcooling method?
    a. never   b. when recommended by the manufacturer
    c. always   d. when the outdoor temp is below 70° F

9. Checking the charge by restricting the condenser fan airflow, while the system is running in cooling mode, will not be accurate if...
    a. the indoor DB temp is below 70° F.   b. the system has a TXV.
    c. the outdoor ambient temp is below 70° F.   d. the system is a heat pump.

10. In order to read the superheat during air conditioning mode without refrigerant gauges, which of these must happen first?

    a. the outdoor coil box's front cover needs to be removed while the system is off

    b. the outdoor coil box's front cover needs to be removed while the system is running

    c. the indoor coil box's front cover needs to be removed while the system is running

    d. the indoor coil box's front cover needs to be removed while the system is off

11. In order to read the superheat without pressure gauges, one bead temp sensor needs to be mounted to a copper tubing elbow inside the evaporator coil box at the location of what?

    a. the inlet of the piston chamber   b. the outlet of the piston chamber

    c. the TXV   d. the saturated state

12. Where does the second bead temp sensor need to be connected to the vapor line in order to read the superheat without pressure gauges?

    a. the middle of the condenser   b. right after the evaporator coil

    c. right after the condenser   d. right before the evaporator coil

Note: The following methods <u>should not</u> be used to check the refrigerant charge on a heat pump or air conditioner in cooling mode.

Fill in the blanks with the correct word(s).

13. The Ambient _____ Rule refers to 10 seer units.

14. The Ambient _____ Rule refers to 13 seer units.

15. Seeing if the vapor line is _____.

16. Feeling how _____ the _____ line with your hand.

17. _____ T

18. Setting the _____ for the low side or high side depending on the outdoor _____ and personal experience.

19. Targeting a 40° F _____ temperature on the _____ side.

Circle the correct bold term(s).

20. Total superheat and subcooling methods can be used for quick **diagnosis / evacuation** when the system does not seem to be working efficiently or properly.

21. **Pressure testing / Delta T** should be used in conjunction with total superheat and subcooling readings when checking the charge and troubleshooting.

22. Charging a system until it is at 40° F saturated temperature on the low side can easily **overcharge / undercharge** the system.

23. Total superheat and subcooling readings can be used to "check the **pressure /charge**".

24. Total superheat and subcooling readings can be used to check the overall system efficiency and to determine if any **moisture / heat transfer** problems exist.

25. When using the Ambient +30 Rule, the outdoor ambient temperature is measured and then 30° F is **added / subtracted** to it to determine the target saturated temperature on the high side of the system.

26. Neither the Ambient +25 Rule nor the Ambient +30 Rule take into consideration measurements taken on the **high / low** side of the system.

27. The Ambient +30 Rule **does / does not** consider any high side fin deterioration.

Circle T for True or F for False.

28. **T / F** Relying on the Ambient +30 Rule may lead to low superheat which can damage the compressor.

29. **T / F** Relying on the Ambient +30 Rule may lead to high superheat and low effeciency.

30. **T / F** The vapor line always sweats on systems that are accurately charged.

31. **T / F** When the suction line is at a lower temperature than the hot, humid air surrounding it, the vapor line sweats.

32. **T / F** The vapor line may not sweat if the indoor wet bulb temp is too high.

33. **T / F** When the vapor line sweats this indicates that the system is running efficiently.

Match the left hand column items with those in the right hand column.

34. _____ A vapor line that feels cold to the touch does not...

35. _____ If there is 0° F of actual superheat, then the refrigerant is still in the saturated state which...

36. _____ There are no normal high side pressures for systems due to various factors. Some of these are...

37. _____ Low side pressures vary depending on...

a. indoor airflow, indoor heat load, the metering device, and other factors.

b. outdoor unit size, deterioration of fins, and outdoor ambient temp.

c. allows both vapor and liquid refrigerant to enter the compressor and results in compressor damage or burnout.

d. always mean the system is accurately charged or running efficiently.

Answer the following with complete sentences.

38. What is the most important reason why using the outdoor ambient temperature and personal experience should not be used to set the pressure for the low or high side?

_____

_____

_____

39. During air conditioning mode, how is the Delta T measured and what is the formula?_____

_____

_____

_____

40. On single and two speed air conditioning systems, a Delta T of 18° F to 21° F is a good sign, but in what scenarios could a system have 18° F to 21° F and still be running inefficiently?

_____

_____

41. On single and two speed air conditioning systems, a Delta T of less than 18° F to 21° F is not usually a good sign, but in what scenario could a system be correctly charged and functioning normally with a Delta T of less than 18° F to 21° F? _____

_____

_____

Circle the correct bold term(s).

42. The saturated temperature on the low side of the system varies **depending on / regardless of** the changing indoor WB and outdoor DB temperatures.

43. The low side saturated temperature on a system with a **fixed orifice / TXV** will vary greatly.

44. The low side saturated temperature on a system with a **fixed orifice / TXV** will only vary slightly.

45. If refrigerant is added to the system to increase the saturated temperature on the low side, the **fixed orifice / TXV** may not allow the saturated temperature to rise.

CHAPTER 13
Troubleshooting an Air Conditioning System

Circle T for True or F for False.

1. **T / F** Prior to attaching the manifold gauge set, the indoor airflow should be checked.

2. **T / F** First, check the windows, doors, and attic entrance to make sure everything is sealed if the system does not seem to be cooling the building.

3. **T / F** Check to see if the air filter is clean. Do this while the system is running.

4. **T / F** A visual check of the condition and size of the outdoor unit, the indoor unit, and the outside of the ducts is usually done prior to troubleshooting a system.

5. **T / F** The capacity of the system, duct size, supply registers and return grilles do not need to be visually checked prior to troubleshooting.

6. **T / F** The indoor airflow volume should match the capacity of the outdoor unit and indoor coil.

7. **T / F** Before measuring the refrigerant charge, make sure the outdoor and indoor temp are both 70° F or above.

Fill in the blanks with the correct word(s).

8. On an air conditioner, a _____ evaporator coil could be the result of a liquid line restriction, low indoor airflow, or a low refrigerant charge.

9. If the evaporator is already frozen, the ice on it needs to be completely melted before turning on the _____ to diagnose the problem.

10. On an air conditioning system, If the sat temp of the refrigerant on the low side gauge does not rise above 32° F after the first _____ minutes of run time, a problem exists which will cause the _____ _____ crossing the outside of the evaporator coil to freeze.

11. Indicators of a low indoor airflow problem with a **TXV** are vapor sat temp _____ 32° F, _____ superheat, normal to _____ subcooling.

12. Indicators of a low indoor airflow problem with a **fixed orifice** are a sat temp _____ 32° F, _____ superheat, normal to _____ subcooling.

13. Indicators of a low refrigerant charge problem with a **TXV** are vapor sat temp below 32° F, _____ to high superheat, and _____ subcooling.

14. Indicators of a low refrigerant charge problem with a **fixed orifice** are vapor sat temp below 32° F, _____ superheat, and _____ subcooling.

15. List 8 causes of low indoor airflow.

_____   _____

_____   _____

_____   _____

_____   _____

16. A _____ action is when the refrigerant pressures dramatically rise and fall back and forth as the TXV tries to maintain its set superheat while not having a steady stream of liquid entering it.

Circle the correct bold term(s).

17. If an air conditioning system worked correctly in the past, but now is not, the system may be low on refrigerant due to **a leak / refrigerant being used up**.

18. Indicators of a liquid line restriction are vapor sat temp below 32° F, **high / low** superheat, and **high / low** subcooling in a system.

19. A liquid line restriction may be the result of a clog in the **accumulator / strainer.**

20. A liquid line restriction may be the result of a bad TXV that has failed toward the **closed / open** position such as when a TXV loses its bulb charge.

Circle T for True or F for False.

21. **T / F** The filter drier is not clogged if the temp downstream of the filter drier is substantially lower than the upstream temp.

22. **T / F** A low airflow problem on a system with a fixed orifice will damage the compressor more severely than a system with a TXV.

23. **T / F** If a system is overcharged, this leads to a higher discharge pressure, higher electrical usage, and a lower lifespan for the compressor.

24. **T / F** As more refrigerant is added to an overcharged system with a TXV, the total superheat and subcooling both decrease.

25. **T / F** If a system with a fixed orifice if overcharged, the superheat will be higher and the subcooling will be lower than normal.

26. **T / F** If the system has a low subcooling, the system's pressures will be higher than normal.

27. **T / F** When there is a few degrees of total superheat, saturated refrigerant will enter the vapor compressor.

28. **T / F** While a system is running, the actual superheat of the system fluctuates depending on the indoor WB and outdoor DB temps.

29. **T / F** Compressor failure will occur if refrigerant is added into a system until there is no superheat.

30. **T / F** Excessive high side pressure leads to a decrease in electrical efficiency.

31. **T / F** Indicators of a refrigerant charge that is contaminated with air or nitrogen are high superheat, high subcooling, and high vapor saturated temp.

Circle the best answer for each statement/question.

32. Systems are labeled with the type of refrigerant the manufacturer designed it for. Where is the type of refrigerant usually listed on the system?

    a. the compressor housing   b. the outdoor unit rating plate

    c. the TXV   d. All of the above

33. With the system off and the pressures equalized, which of the following indicates the refrigerant charge is not contaminated?

    a. Refrigerant converted to sat temp > outdoor ambient temp

    b. Refrigerant converted to sat temp = outdoor ambient temp

    c. Refrigerant converted to sat temp < outdoor ambient temp

    d. None of the above

34. With the system off and the pressures equalized, which of the following indicates that a different refrigerant or an extremely low charge is in the system?

    a. Refrigerant converted to sat temp > outdoor ambient temp

    b. Refrigerant converted to sat temp = outdoor ambient temp

    c. Refrigerant converted to sat temp < outdoor ambient temp

    d. None of the above

35. With the system off and the pressures equalized, which of the following indicates a different refrigerant is in the system or that air or nitrogen are mixed with the refrigerant?

    a. Refrigerant converted to sat temp > outdoor ambient temp

    b. Refrigerant converted to sat temp = outdoor ambient temp

    c. Refrigerant converted to sat temp < outdoor ambient temp

    d. None of the above

Circle the correct bold term(s).

36. Very high vapor pressure in an air conditioning system may be caused by **leaking compressor valves / a clogged filter drier.**

37. A **internal pressure relief valve / reversing valve** may not move or seal properly if the unit is low on refrigerant.

38. TXV bulb charge lost = **High / Low** superheat and **High / Low** subcooling

39. If the bulb loses its refrigerant charge, the TXV will allow **less / more** refrigerant into the evaporator coil.

Circle T for True or F for False.

40. **T / F** If a reciprocating compressor is suspected of having bad valves and the unit does not have a Micro-Channel coil, the problem can be diagnosed by performing a partial pump down procedure.

41. **T / F** If the pressures on the vapor and liquid lines go down during a pump down, but then a loud noise occurs and the pressures rise, the problem is the TXV.

42. **T / F** On a heat pump in cooling mode, a faulty reversing valve may cause overly high vapor pressure.

43. **T / F** A reversing valve may not move or seal properly if the unit is low on refrigerant.

44. **T / F** A clogged TXV is considered a liquid line restriction.

45. **T / F** A TXV stuck in the open position is considered a liquid line restriction.

Match the left hand column items with those in the right hand column.

46. _____ A liquid line restriction may be caused by...

a. on the vapor line at the outlet of the evaporator coil.

47. _____ If the TXV bulb is placed in hot water and the low side pressure rises and the superheat decreases...

b. the bulb is low on refrigerant but there is still some refrigerant in the bulb.

48. _____ The TXV bulb should be located...

49. _____ Use either two stainless steel hose clamps or two copper straps with brass nuts and bolts to secure...

c. the refrigerant inside the bulb is at the same temp as the refrigerant in the vapor line.

d. a clogged filter drier or screen before the TXV.

50. _____ Insulate over both the vapor tube and the bulb so that...

e. the bulb correctly to the vapor line.

Use the Troubleshooting Guide (Figure 13-13 on page 178 of the textbook) to diagnose the problem based on the indicators listed for each question.

51. If an air conditioning system has a TXV with a partially frozen evaporator, low vapor sat temp, low liquid sat temp, normal superheat, and normal to high subcooling, what is the problem?

_____

52. The air conditioning system has a piston and the superheat and subcooling are both high. Delta T, vapor sat temp, capacity and compressor amps are all low. The liquid sat temp is normal to low and there is some freezing at the evaporator. What is the problem?

_____

The following questions are in reference to a frozen evaporator coil. Fill in the blanks based on the image and determine if the problem is a <u>low refrigerant charge</u>, <u>liquid line restriction</u>, or <u>low indoor airflow</u>. Use the Troubleshooting Guide (Figure 13-13 on page 178 of the textbook) to determine the problem.

53. **R-410A** unit with <u>TXV</u>

   a. Vapor sat temp: _____

   b. Actual temp on the vapor line: _____

   c. Actual total superheat: _____

   d. Liquid sat temp: _____

   e. Actual temp on the liquid line: _____

   f. Actual subcooling: _____

   g. Problem: _____

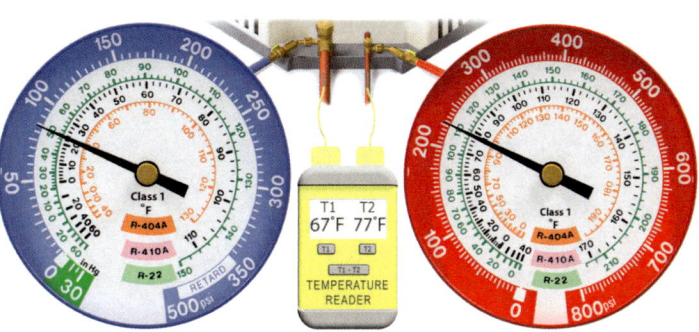

54. **R-410A** unit with <u>Piston</u>

   a. Vapor sat temp: _____

   b. Actual temp on the vapor line: _____

   c. Actual total superheat: _____

   d. Liquid sat temp: _____

   e. Actual temp on the liquid line: _____

   f. Actual subcooling: _____

   g. Problem: _____

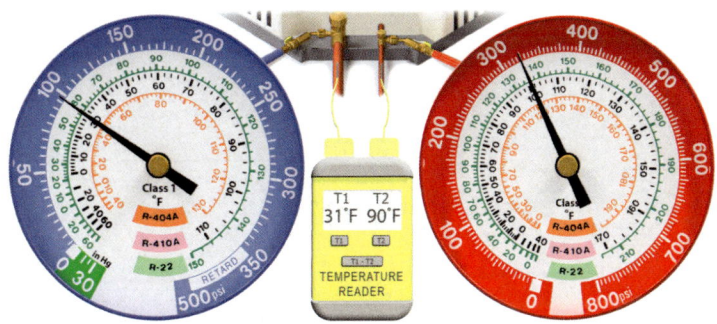

55. **R-410A** unit with <u>Piston</u>

   a. Vapor sat temp: _____

   b. Actual temp on the vapor line: _____

   c. Actual total superheat: _____

   d. Liquid sat temp: _____

   e. Actual temp on the liquid line: _____

   f. Actual subcooling: _____

   g. Problem: _____

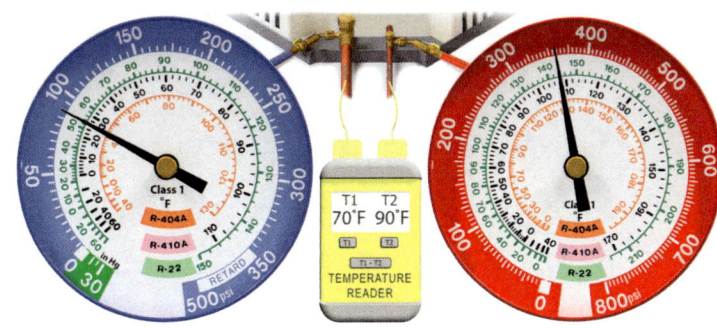

56. **R-410A** unit with <u>TXV</u>

   a. Vapor sat temp: _____

   b. Actual temp on the vapor line: _____

   c. Actual total superheat: _____

   d. Liquid sat temp: _____

   e. Actual temp on the liquid line: _____

   f. Actual subcooling: _____

   g. Problem: _____

Fill in the blanks based on the image and use the Troubleshooting Guide (Figure 13-13 on page 178 of the textbook) to determine the problem.

---

57. **R-410A** unit with **TXV**

    a. Vapor sat temp: _____

    b. Actual temp on the vapor line: _____

    c. Actual total superheat: _____

    d. Liquid sat temp: _____

    e. Actual temp on the liquid line: _____

    f. Actual subcooling: _____

    g. Problem: _____

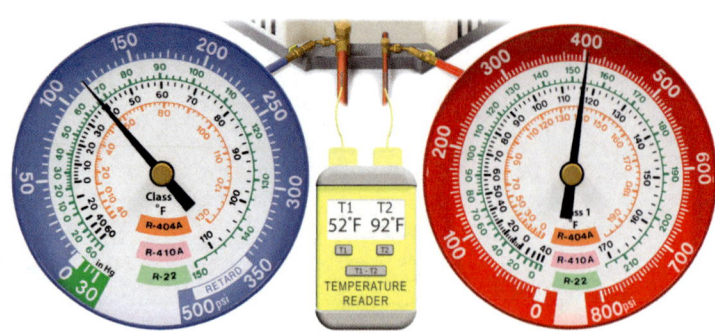

58. **R-410A** unit with **TXV**

    a. Vapor sat temp: _____

    b. Actual temp on the vapor line: _____

    c. Actual total superheat: _____

    d. Liquid sat temp: _____

    e. Actual temp on the liquid line: _____

    f. Actual subcooling: _____

    g. Problem: _____

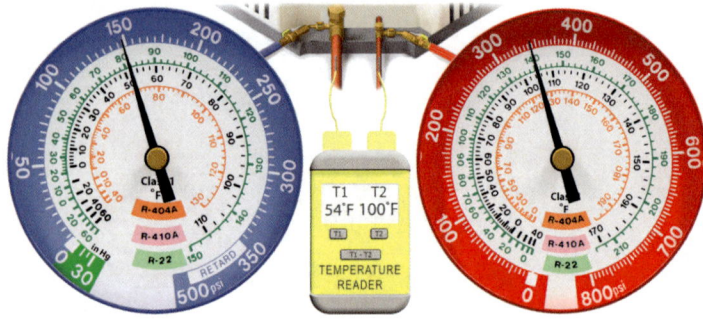

59. **R-22** unit with **Piston**

    a. Vapor sat temp: _____

    b. Actual temp on the vapor line: _____

    c. Actual total superheat: _____

    d. Liquid sat temp: _____

    e. Actual temp on the liquid line: _____

    f. Actual subcooling: _____

    g. Problem: _____

60. **R-22** unit with **Piston**

    a. Vapor sat temp: _____

    b. Actual temp on the vapor line: _____

    c. Actual total superheat: _____

    d. Liquid sat temp: _____

    e. Actual temp on the liquid line: _____

    f. Actual subcooling: _____

    g. Problem: _____

CHAPTER 14
Poor System Installation or Design Problems that May be Encountered

Circle T for True or F for False.

1. **T / F** A TXV that is manufactured for one refrigerant can be used in a system that contains another refrigerant only if both refrigerants have a very similar boiling point.

2. **T / F** R-410A and R-22 are two refrigerants with similar boiling points.

3. **T / F** To determine the correct BTU/HR capacity of a system for a building, a heat load and loss calculation must be performed on the building.

4. **T / F** An undersized TXV will result in high superheat.

5. **T / F** An undersized piston will result in low superheat.

6. **T / F** An oversized piston will result in high superheat

7. **T / F** The capacity of a system's evaporator coil, metering device, and outdoor unit must match in order for the system to work properly.

Circle the best answer for each statement/question.

8. Which of these will determine the line set size that is needed?

    a. length and rise of line set   b. BTU/HR capacity

    c. oil and refrigerant   d. All of the above

9. In order to find the target superheat for a system, take readings of...

    a. DB and WB temps inside.   b. a WB temp outside and a DB temp inside.

    c. DB and WB temps outside.   d. a DB temp outside and a WB temp inside.

10. Which of these **will not** cause damage to the refrigerant compressor when entering it?

    a. liquid refrigerant   b. saturated refrigerant

    c. vapor refrigerant   d. acid

11. When installing an air conditioning system in a dry climate, which of these is best to install for efficiency and compressor protection?

    a. piston metering device   b. capillary metering device

    c. suction line filter drier   d. TXV metering device

Answer the following with complete sentences.

12. Can an R-22 TXV be used in an R-410A system? Why or why not? _____

_____

_____

13. Can an R-22 TXV be used in an R-407C system? Why or why not? _____

_____

_____

14. Compared to a piston, what are the advantage(s) of installing a TXV in a new split system? _____

_____

_____

15. How can water accidentally enter a system and mix with the refrigerant oil? Discuss two instances.

_____

_____

_____

16. What is the chemical result of water and refrigerant oil mixing together, and what effect does this have

on a system? _____

_____

_____

Circle the correct bold term(s).

17. If acid is found in a system, it is crucial to add **a detergent / an oil treatment** to the system to chemically

bond to the acid or to neutralize it.

18. Use an acid **ultrasonic detector / test kit** to determine if a high acid level is present in the system.

19. A telltale sign of an acid problem is **vapor gas escaping / oil bubbling** after the refrigerant hose is

disconnected from the service port.

20. A high acid level that is not dealt with will likely cause the **compressor / receiver** to burn out.

21. An **undersized / oversized** evaporator coil with a piston sized to the outdoor unit capacity may result in

low superheat and compressor damage.

22. An **oversized / undersized** TXV may result in low superheat and / or compressor damage.

CHAPTER 15
Troubleshooting Low Airflow Problems

Fill in the blanks with the correct word(s).

1. CFM= _____ _____ per _____

2. The indoor airflow CFM should be measured and compared to the _____ size of the system prior to checking the refrigerant charge.

3. If there is an insufficient amount of airflow compared to the BTU/HR size of the system, then the _____ _____ may freeze, the system may run inefficiently, and the _____ may be damaged.

4. 1 ton = _____BTU/HR = roughly _____ CFM of airflow.

5. _____ ton(s) = _____BTU/HR = roughly 1200 CFM of airflow.

6. For a building with high humidity, the system can be set to run at _____CFM per 1 ton of cooling capacity to lower the humidity effectively.

Match the left hand column items with those in the right hand column.

7. _____ A Rotating Vane Anemometer

8. _____ Traversing the Duct

9. _____ Flow Capture Hood

10. _____ Timed Inflation

a. This method uses either a dual port manometer and a long Pitot tube or a hot wire anemometer.

b. This device has a large opening which covers the return grille or supply register.

c. This small hand held device has a fan blade that measures airflow.

d. This method utilizes the time it takes to inflate a bag when it is covering a supply air register.

Circle T for True or F for False.

11. **T / F** The TESP stands for Total Exiting Static Pressure.

12. **T / F** Static pressure is the amount of pressure measured in inches of WC (Water Column) that a blower motor must use to move air through an object.

13. **T / F** The TESP measures the combined static pressure of only the filter and return duct.

14. **T / F** It is possible to determine if there is an overall problem affecting airflow by measuring the TESP on an operating packaged unit, an air handler or a furnace.

15. **T / F** A dual anemometer with a negative and positive port can be used to measure the actual TESP of a furnace.

16. **T / F** Since a furnace is shipped with the furnace heat exchanger inside, the heat exchanger is not included in the max TESP.

17. **T / F** If an air handler is shipped with a filter inside, the filter is included in the max TESP.

18. **T / F** The heat exchanger and evaporator coil are included in the max TESP of a packaged unit.

19. **T / F** If the actual TESP is higher than the max TESP rating of the unit, the individual return and supply side static pressure readings can be used to start pinpointing the problem.

Match the left hand column items with those in the right hand column.

20. _____ The CFM across an electrical resistance heater can be determined using this method by measuring voltage, amperage, and temperature.

a. [138,500 x (GPH of nozzle) x (Combustion Efficiency)] / (1.08 x Delta T)

21. _____ Temporarily use the cooling mode air speed during heating mode while the measurements are taken to...

b. determine the cooling airflow volume using the Temp Rise Formula

c. a flow capture hood

22. _____ The Temp Rise Formula used on a natural gas or propane furnace =

d. (Input BTU/HR x Combustion Efficiency) / (1.08 x Delta T)

23. _____ The Temp Rise Formula used on a fuel oil furnace =

24. _____ The Temp Rise Formula used on an air handler with electrical resistance heat =

e. (Volts x Amps x 3.414) / (1.08 x Delta T)

25. _____ A tool that quickly measures airflow by covering over the supply register or return grille

f. the Temp Rise Formula

26. _____ A tool that measures airflow as it is moved across the face of an opening, register, or grille

g. Hot Wire Anemometer

27. _____ A tool that is capable of measuring airflow through test ports in the duct

h. Rotating Vane Anemometer

Circle the correct bold term(s).

28. The most common airflow setting is **500 / 400** CFM per 12,000 BTU/HR.

29. If the evaporator coil next to the furnace is clogged with dust, this will result in a high static pressure on the **return / supply** side.

30. If the air filter is clogged, this will result in a high static pressure on the **return / supply** side.

31. **TESP / Static pressure** readings can be taken across individual components to pinpoint the airflow restriction.

32. If the pressure drop across an air filter is **abnormally high / slightly low**, the filter should be replaced.

33. Compare the static pressure drop across the component with the **manufacturer's / slide rule** data.

Use each image to solve the following questions.

34. Determine the CFM of this running air handler equipped with electric strip heaters using the Temp Rise Method. Show your work using the equation found in the book.

    Strip heater voltage = 241 Volts, Strip heater current = 21 amps

    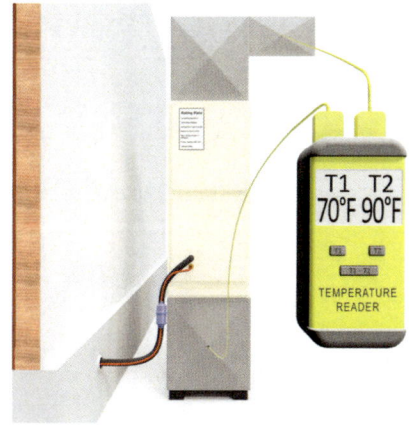

    _____

    _____

    CFM= _____

35. What is the Total External Static Pressure measured on this system?

    _____ " WC

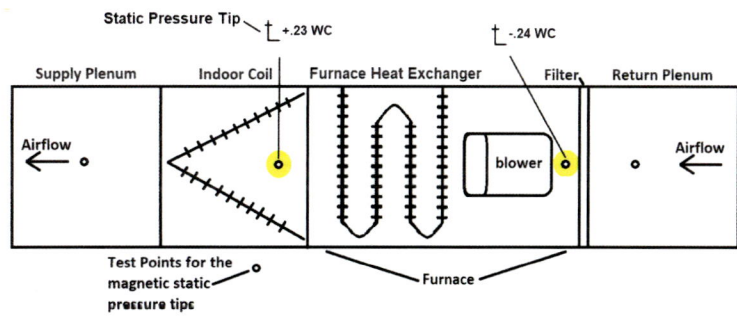

36. This system is running at an airflow of 800 CFM in air conditioning mode. The literature from the manufacturer of the indoor coil shows the wet coil static pressure should be .18 WC at 800 CFM. Is this coil partially <u>clogged</u> or <u>clean</u>? What is the static pressure drop across the coil? _____ " WC

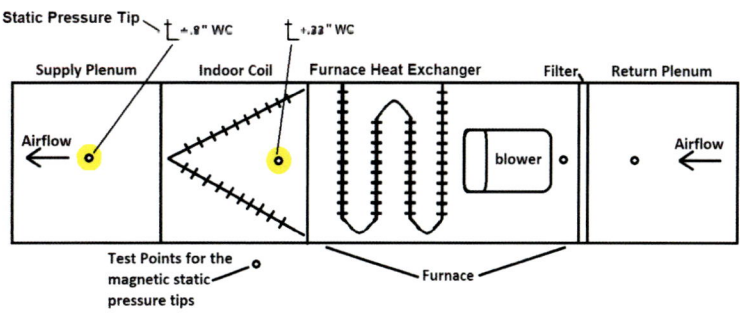

CHAPTER 16
Metering Devices

Circle T for True or F for False.

1. **T / F** The liquid refrigerant's pressure is lowered by the metering device.

2. **T / F** The refrigerant changes phase from a vapor to a liquid after the metering device in the coil.

3. **T / F** The piston, capillary tube, and TXV are the three most common metering devices.

4. **T / F** The TXV is a fixed orifice metering device.

5. **T / F** In order to prevent a capillary tube from being clogged, a cylindrical strainer is usually installed so the liquid refrigerant passes through it before entering the capillary tube.

Label the following images.

6. Label **a** through **f**.

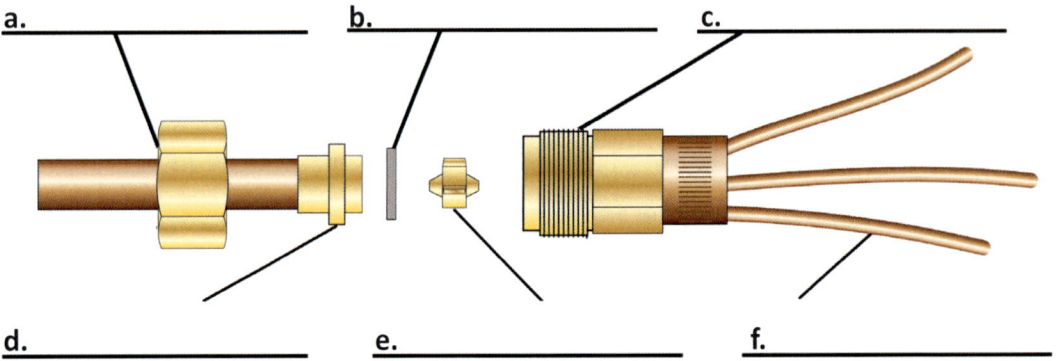

a. _____ b. _____ c. _____

d. _____ e. _____ f. _____

7. Label **a** through **j**.   8. Label **a** through **c** as P1, P2, or P3

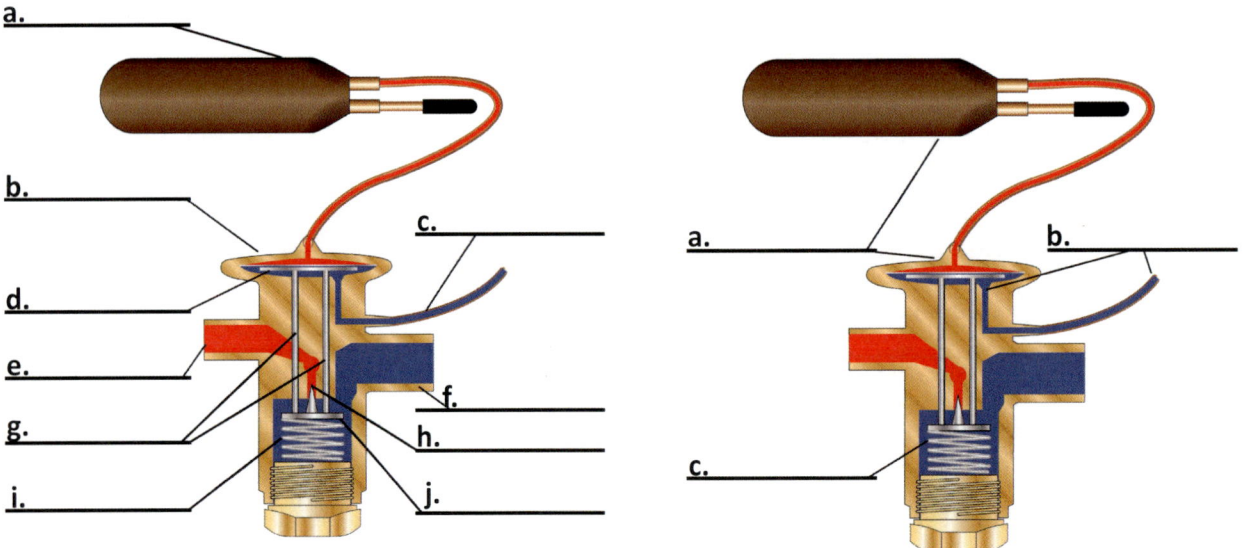

a. _____

b. _____ c. _____

d. _____

e. _____

g. _____ f. _____

i. _____ h. _____

j. _____

a. _____ b. _____

c. _____

Circle the best answer for each statement/question.

9. Which of these are fixed orifices?

    a. TXV and capillary tubing   b. TXV and piston

    c. capillary tubing and piston   d. capillary tubing, piston, TXV

10. Capillary tubing is commonly used as a metering device in which of these?

    a. window ac units   b. heat pumps

    c. walk in freezers   d. All of the above

11. A piston has a hole size diameter that must be matched with the refrigerant type and...

    a. subcooling value.   b. the length of the line set.

    c. BTU/HR capacity of the system.   d. All of the above

12. Which of these is *false* in reference to a piston metering device and piston chamber.

    a. the piston hole size changes based   b. the piston chamber can be opened to
        on the present superheat   replace the piston

    c. pistons that are made by the same   d. depending on the directional flow of the refrigerant,
        manufacturer are interchangeable   the piston can slide back and forth inside the chamber

13. Which of the following is *not* a reason why manufacturers build a piston chamber onto the evaporator coil?

    a. pistons are interchangeable   b. it allows the piston a bypass function when
                                      refrigerant changes direction

    c. pistons are more energy efficient   d. the evaporator coil can be built for either a piston
        than TXVs   metering device in the chamber or a TXV mounted

                                          on the chamber

Fill in the blanks with the correct word(s).

14. The _____ tubes feed the refrigerant from the metering device into the evaporator coil.

15. If the piston installed in the chamber is too large for the system capacity, then the evaporator coil will have little or no _____.

16. If the piston installed in the chamber is too small for the system capacity, then the evaporator coil will have high _____.

17. If the piston installed in the chamber is too large for the system capacity, then the _____ will be in danger of having _____ refrigerant entering in.

18. TXV stands for _____ _____ _____.

19. A TXV can change the size of its metering _____.

Match the left hand column items with those in the right hand column.

20. _____ On a heat pump in cooling mode, the   a. during a high heat load

     piston in the liquid line at the indoor

     coil is referred to as this.   b. the active metering device

21. _____ On a heat pump in heating mode, the

     piston in the liquid line at the indoor   c. the TXV adjusts the amount of liquid

     coil is referred to as this.   refrigerant going through it

22. _____ This is when the TXV lets in less refrigerant.

23. _____ This is when the TXV lets in more refrigerant.   d. during a low heat load

24. _____ In order to keep the superheat as

     constant as possible this happens.   e. the inactive metering device

Circle the correct bold term(s).

25. Most newer TXV's are equipped with an **external / internal** bypass valve which allows the metering

     device mounted on the indoor coil to become **active / inactive** during heating mode.

26. Refrigeration TXV's are usually **adjustable / nonadjustable.**

27. The spring pressure can be adjusted by accessing the **bulb / stem** after removing the seal cap off the

     bottom of the TXV.

28. Decreasing the spring pressure **decreases / increases** the superheat.

29. Increasing the spring pressure **decreases / increases** the superheat.

30. A TXV is **adjustable / nonadjustable** if it has a flat bottom without a cap.

31. The sensing bulb is connected to the power head of a TXV via a **capillary / line set** tube.

32. Heat transfers to the sensing bulb from direct contact with the **liquid / vapor** line set tube.

Circle T for True or F for False.

33. **T / F** The sensing bulb is mounted to the tube using either copper or stainless steel straps or clamps.

34. **T / F** The sensing bulb needs to be in contact with a straight, clean section of liquid tube.

35. **T / F** When mounting the sensing bulb vertically, the tubes coming out of the bulb must be faced

     downward.

36. **T / F** The bulb pressure pushes down on the diaphragm that pushes down on the internal pin.

37. **T / F** Each TXV metering device has both an internal and an external equalizer.

38. **T / F** An internally equalized TXV is usually used on systems that have distributor tubes.

39. **T / F** The equalizer pressure pushes up on the diaphragm and therefore up on the internal pin.

Circle the best answer for each statement/question.

40. Which tool should be used to adjust the spring pressure on a TXV?

    a. valve core tool
    b. torque wrench
    c. ratcheting service wrench
    d. None of the above

41. The spring pressure is a closing force that pushes up on the diaphragm and is referred to as...

    a. P1.
    b. P2.
    c. P3.
    d. P1 + P2.

42. The equalizer pressure is a closing force that pushes up on the diaphragm and is referred to as...

    a. P1.
    b. P2.
    c. P3.
    d. P1 + P3.

43. The bulb pressure is an opening force that pushes down on the diaphragm and is referred to as...

    a. P1.
    b. P2.
    c. P3.
    d. P2 + P3.

44. A TXV is set to maintain a certain _____ across the evaporator coil.

    a. subcooling
    b. total superheat
    c. superheat
    d. wet bulb temperature

45. The TXV bulb mounting position typically should be...

    a. on the external equalizer line.
    b. upstream from the external equalizer.
    c. downstream from the external equalizer.
    d. on the liquid line.

Fill in the blanks with the correct word(s).

46. When the TXV bulb is mounted on a vertical tube, the capillary tubing on the bulb must be faced

    _____.

47. When the horizontal _____ line is large in diameter, mount the bulb on

    the side of the tube at roughly 3 o'clock or 9 o'clock.

48. When the horizontal _____ line has an OD of 7/8" or less, the bulb can

    be mounted higher at _____ o'clock or _____ o'clock.

49. A _____ orifice allows the same amount of refrigerant through even if the heat load changes at

    the evaporator coil.

50. EEV stands for _____ _____ _____.

51. AEV stands for _____ _____ _____.

52. A liquid line restriction may be caused by a bad TXV, a clogged _____, or a clogged

    _____ _____.

53. If a TXV fails, it usually fails in the partially _____ position.

54. When a TXV fails as described in the previous problem, the vapor pressure is low, the Delta T is low,

    and the _____ and _____ are both high.

55. A _____ is a valve that is actuated by powering an electrical coil mounted on it.

Match the left hand column items with those in the right hand column.

56. _____ The EEV is used on high efficiency
        systems...

57. _____ The AEV is typically used in packaged units...

58. _____ Since there is no bulb attached to the
        head of this type of valve...

59. _____ When a TXV metering device is in a system...

60. _____ The TXV limits the amount of refrigerant
        entering the evaporator coil when...

a. a low airflow situation is caused by
   a clogged air filter or a collapsed duct.

b. it is easy to identify an AEV.

c. where multiple sensors are used to measure
   operating conditions.

d. use the subcooling method to check the
   charge.

e. where operating parameters and heat
   loads are fairly consistent.

CHAPTER 17
HVAC System Components

Circle T for True or F for False.

1. **T / F** Scroll, rotary, and reciprocating compressors are the main types of compressors used in light commercial and residential air conditioning systems.

2. **T / F** Centrifugal and screw compressors are used in small refrigerators, RV air conditioners, and window air conditioners.

3. **T / F** Compressors can be open-drive, semi-hermetic, or hermetically sealed.

4. **T / F** Refrigerant oil and the refrigerant circulate separately through the system.

5. **T / F** The refrigerant oil lubricates the compressor.

6. **T / F** Compressor and equipment manufacturers do not recommend to pump down systems with a reciprocating or rotary compressor but do allow for a pump down of a scroll compressor.

7. **T / F** Refrigerant vapor acts as insulation between the electrical windings and the ground frame in a scroll compressor.

Match the left hand column items with those in the right hand column.

8. _____ Reciprocating compressor   a. has few moving parts and compresses the refrigerant by orbiting the bottom part against the fixed top part

9. _____ Rotary compressor   b. has a crankshaft with one or more pistons

10. _____ Scroll compressor   c. has a cylindrical roller that compresses the refrigerant into a small area

Fill in the blanks with the correct word(s).

11. The refrigerant oil type and amount is determined by the manufacturer as stated on the rating plate and weighed into the unit at the _____.

12. Because of the certain refrigerants used in residential air conditioning systems, most common lubricants presently found in these systems are _____ _____ and _____ oil.

13. Mineral oil is matched with many HCFC and CFC refrigerants due to their _____.

Circle the best answer for each statement/question.

14. Hermetic means which of these?

      a. The motor and the compressor pump are separate and connected together via a shaft.

      b. The motor and pump are sealed inside a welded steel shell.

      c. The motor and pump are sealed in a shell with a mix of gaskets and welds.

      d. None of the above

15. Semi-hermetic means which of these?

      a. The motor and the compressor pump are separate and connected together via a shaft.

      b. The motor and pump are sealed inside a welded steel shell.

      c. The motor and pump are sealed in a shell with a mix of gaskets and welds.

      d. None of the above

16. Open-drive means which of these?

      a. The motor and the compressor pump are separate and connected together via a shaft.

      b. The motor and pump are sealed inside a welded steel shell.

      c. The motor and pump are sealed in a shell with a mix of gaskets and welds.

      d. None of the above

17. Which compressor always has a unique type of accumulator mounted on the suction side?

      a. reciprocating   b. scroll   c. rotary   d. All of the above

18. Which compressor was originally the most common type used in residential and light commercial air conditioning units?

      a. reciprocating   b. scroll   c. rotary   d. screw

Answer the Following.

19. State the oil type for each of the following abbreviations

      a. MO = _____

      b. POE= _____

      c. AKB= _____

      d. PAG= _____

20. Define miscibility as it pertains to refrigerants and refrigerant oil. Explain why it is important.

      _____

      _____

      _____

21. What two things does the rating plate indicate about the refrigerant oil in a unit? _____

_____

22. Give an example of an HCFC refrigerant that is miscible with mineral oil. _____

23. Give an example of an HFC refrigerant that is miscible with POE. _____

24. What happens when water mixes with refrigerant oil? How can this negatively affect the seals, as well as the electrical windings inside the compressor of a system? _____

_____

_____

_____

Circle the correct bold term(s).

25. Mineral oil is **more / less** hygroscopic than POE oil.

26. Hygroscopic means easily **combines with / separates from** water.

27. A compressor burnout can devastate a system because it leaves a burnt **carbon / hygroscopic** residue throughout the inner walls of the tubing inside the system.

28. If a compressor burnout occurs, clean the **line set / coil fins** and any other tubing before replacing components in the system.

29. If the system is located outside, the system's refrigerant charge should not be accessed when it is **raining / hot** and humid.

Circle T for True or F for False.

30. **T / F** Water mixed with refrigerant oil will create acid and/or alcohol.

31. **T / F** A filter drier has an unlimited capacity for trapping water in the system.

32. **T / F** If the filter drier is clogged, there will be a pressure drop across it.

33. **T / F** Besides water, the liquid line filter drier can also trap solid contaminants and acids from the refrigerant charge.

34. **T / F** An acid neutralizer must not be used to reduce the acidity of the oil on systems with a reciprocating compressor.

35. **T / F** Any time an existing system is opened to atmospheric pressure, the filter drier must be replaced.

Match the left hand column items with those in the right hand column.

36. _____ Verify that the filter drier is rated for the type of refrigerant being used...

    a. prior to a capillary tube metering device.

37. _____ Heat pump systems need a bi-flow filter drier in order to...

    b. in the system prior to installing it.

38. _____ Make sure to cut out sweat-on-filter driers...

    c. allow for the replacement of the exchangeable core.

39. _____ A copper spun filter drier may be installed in a location...

    d. so that moisture is not accidentally released into the system.

40. _____ Large commercial non-hermetically sealed filter driers...

    e. allow the system's refrigerant to flow in either direction.

Circle the best answer for each statement/question.

41. What are the vapor and liquid tubes on a split system that connect the indoor unit to the outdoor unit called?

    a. return lines   b. indoor and outdoor lines

    c. line set   d. All of the above

42. Which of these affect the diameter of the line set required on a system?

    a. refrigerant type   b. compressor and oil types

    c. the line length, rise and drop   d. All of the above

43. On an air conditioner, the vapor line tube connects the vapor line service valve at the compressor inlet to the vapor line from the...

    a. evaporator coil.   b. metering device.

    c. internal equalization line.   d. condenser coil.

44. On an air conditioner, the liquid line tube connects the outdoor unit liquid line service valve to the...

    a. evaporator coil.   b. metering device.

    c. external equalization line.   d. condenser coil.

Fill in the blanks with the correct word(s).

45. After connecting the line set to a new split system, perform a _____ _____ to check for leaks, _____ the system to remove the air, nitrogen, and water, and then add refrigerant.

46. Line set usually comes in copper coil lengths of 25', 30' and _____. It may be available in longer coils for _____ units.

47. Copper tubing used as line set is referred to as either ACR (_____ _____

    _____) tubing, OD tubing, or annealed temper copper tubing.

48. For conventional split system air conditioners and heat pumps, the large _____ line tube is

    insulated while the small _____ line tube is uninsulated.

49. On _____ systems, both the liquid and the vapor lines need to be insulated

    because they both travel through the building while the refrigerant is at a low temperature.

Circle the correct bold term(s).

50. **1/4 " / 3/8"** ACR tubing is commonly used for the liquid line in residential split systems for either

    R-410A or R-22.

51. For residential air conditioning split systems containing R-22 or R-410A, the vapor line sizes typically

    range from **1/4 " / 5/8"** all the way to 1 1/8" depending on the size of the system and the

    manufacturer's recommendation.

52. The size of residential air conditioning and heat pump units usually do not exceed **48,000 / 60,000**

    BTU/HR.

53. A **Hermetic / Open drive** compressor needs a constant flow of refrigerant to cool the compressor

    motor and oil to lubricate the **winding / pump** assembly.

54. When a system is running, the **liquid / vapor** line carries less refrigerant than the **liquid / vapor** line.

Use the refrigerant weight per foot chart (Figure 17-14 on page 216 of the textbook) to determine the answers for the following questions.

55. An R-407C system is installed with 50' of 3/8" liquid line and 50' of 7/8" vapor line. The manufacturer's

    factory charge of 6 lb 9 oz includes enough refrigerant for 25' of 3/8" and 25' of 7/8" line set. Determine

    how much refrigerant weight needs to be added to the factory charge.

    a. **Show your work.**

    b. **Refrigerant needed for 3/8" liquid line:**_____

    c. **Refrigerant needed for 7/8" vapor line:**_____

    d. **Total amount of extra refrigerant needed:**_____

56. An R-410A system is installed with 40' of 3/8" liquid line and 40' of 3/4" vapor line. The manufacturer's charge of 5 lb 3 oz includes enough refrigerant for 15' of 3/8" and 15' of 3/4" line set. Determine how much extra refrigerant weight needs to be added to the factory charge.

    a. **Show your work.**

    b. **Refrigerant needed for 3/8" liquid line:**_____

    c. **Refrigerant needed for 3/4" vapor line:**_____

    d. **Total amount of extra refrigerant needed:**_____

Answer the following with complete sentences.

57. Where is the evaporator located in the system and what happens to the refrigerant in the evaporator?

    _____

    _____

    _____

58. Where is the condenser located in the system and what happens to the refrigerant in the condenser?

    _____

    _____

    _____

59. On a heat pump system, why is it recommended to ***not*** refer to the coils as the evaporator and condenser?

    _____

    _____

60. What are the functions of an accumulator and where is it installed? _____

    _____

    _____

61. If oil and liquid refrigerant gather at the bottom of the accumulator tank, how are they transported back into the system? _____

    _____

    _____

Circle T for True or F for False.

62. **T / F** An accumulator can be found in both heat pumps and mini-split units.

63. **T / F** Any time a system has a scroll compressor, there is always an accumulator attached to the inlet of the compressor.

64. **T / F** A unit that has the possibility of high superheat being present at the inlet of the compressor will usually have an accumulator installed onto the unit.

65. **T / F** If total superheat is measured at the vapor line near the compressor inlet, this verifies that only vapor is entering the compressor.

Circle the best answer for each statement/question.

66. An accumulator acts like a storage tank for excess refrigerant during heating mode in...

    a. heat pump systems.   b. multi-channel systems.

    c. refrigerators.   d. air conditioning systems.

67. The "4 Way Valve" is another name for a...

    a. bi-flow filter drier.   b. TXV.   c. reversing valve.   d. king valve.

68. The single tube on a 4 Way Valve is always connected to the discharge from the...

    a. condenser.   b. accumulator.

    c. outdoor unit.   d. compressor.

69. On a 4 Way Valve, the center tube on the three tube side is always the...

    a. high pressure vapor.   b. low pressure vapor.

    c. high pressure liquid.   d. low pressure liquid.

Fill in the blanks with the correct word(s).

70. A _____ _____ has two metering devices.

71. On a split type refrigeration system that has a TXV, the _____ is used to store subcooled liquid when the evaporator is operating at a low heat load.

72. The _____ is used to store subcooled liquid in an automatic _____ _____ refrigeration system.

73. The _____ _____ is a 3 position service valve located on the top or side of the receiver.

74. To perform a manual pump down, the flow of liquid refrigerant can be stopped by _____ - seating the king valve.

Match the left hand column items with those in the right hand column.

75. _____ On a reversing valve, the single tube is...

a. typically have a receiver installed on the outdoor unit.

76. _____ On a reversing valve, the center one of the three tubes is...

b. a tank that stores subcooled liquid.

77. _____ The pilot valve controls the U-shaped slide position by...

c. only one metering device is active at a time.

78. _____ On a heat pump system...

d. using refrigerant pressure from the pilot valve tubing.

79. _____ The receiver is...

f. always the suction line going to the accumulator and then to the inlet of the compressor.

80. _____ Split type refrigeration systems that are equipped with a TXV...

e. always connected to the high pressure discharge line.

81. Label the compressor in each image as <u>scroll</u>, <u>rotary</u>, or <u>reciprocating</u>.

a. _____

b. _____

c. _____

82. Label the compressor internals as <u>scroll</u>, <u>rotary</u>, or <u>reciprocating</u>.

a. _____

b. _____

c. _____

83. Label the parts of the reversing valve.

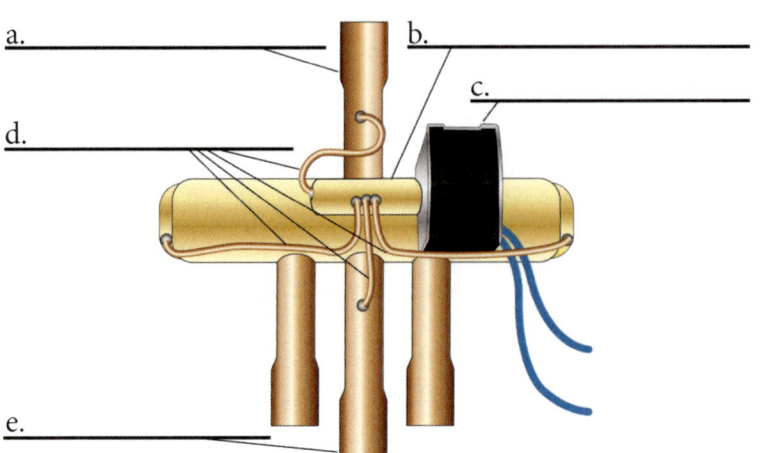

a. _____

b. _____

c. _____

d. _____

e. _____

Appendix A
System Heat Removal Capacity

Circle T for True or F for False.

1. **T / F** A system's heat removal capacity is expressed in BTU/HR.

2. **T / F** A heat load and loss calculation is needed to determine the size of the HVACR system needed for a building.

3. **T / F** Tonnage is another term used to describe the size and weight of an air conditioning system.

4. **T / F** A ton is equal to 2,000 BTU/HR.

5. **T / F** 4 tons of air conditioning equals 42,000 BTU/HR of heat removal capacity.

6. **T / F** A 30,000 BTU/HR air conditioner can be referred to as a 2.5 ton air conditioning unit.

Appendix B
Heat Load and Loss Calculations

Answer the following with complete sentences.

1. What is heat loss? _____

_____

2. What is heat gain? _____

_____

3. State 5 reasons why a heat load and loss calculation is used to determine the size of the HVAC system needed for a building. _____

_____

_____

_____

_____

Circle the best answer for each statement/question.

4. Which of these must match capacity of the system?

    a. indoor coil and outdoor unit   b. metering device

    c. blower motor   d. All of the above

5. What will happen if an undersized system is installed?

    a. it will never shut off during a high heat load condition   b. it will short cycle

    c. electrical usage will decrease   d. All of the above

6. What will happen if an oversized system is installed?

    a. it will never shut off during a high heat load condition   b. it will short cycle

    c. it will only work properly in the spring   d. it will only work properly in the fall

Circle T for True or F for False.

7. **T / F** New indoor blower motors are usually single speed.

8. **T / F** The equipment capacity selected for the system must be lower than the building's heat load and loss calculations.

9. **T / F** Location of the ductwork, window and door sizes, and the R-value of the insulation in the building are three of the many factors used when formulating a heat load and loss calculation.

10. **T / F** A 40,000 BTU/HR furnace that is 92% efficient can be used to heat a home with a heat loss of 38,000 BTU/HR.

11. **T / F** A heat load of 56,000 BTU/HR on the building will require a 5 ton air conditioner.

12. **T / F** By using the heat load and loss calculation, the technician determines that 21,000 BTU/HR of heat removal and 59,000 BTU/HR of heat addition capacity are needed for the building. The technician should install a furnace that has a 60,000 BTU/HR input that is 95% efficient along with a 1.5 ton air conditioner.

Answer the following.

13. The author mentions seventeen major factors that should be considered when calculating a building's heat load and loss. List at least 10 factors.

    _____   _____

    _____   _____

    _____   _____

    _____   _____

Appendix C
Blend Refrigerants

Circle the correct bold term(s).

1. Blends are a mix of **two or more / three or more** single component refrigerants.

2. The temperature swing between the condensing point and boiling point of a Near-Azeotropic or a Zeotropic refrigerant at a constant **pressure / temperature** is referred to as the "temperature **glide / slide**".

3. The temperature glide is due to each single component refrigerant having **a different / the same** boiling point.

4. The temperature glide ranges from the **freezing / dew** point to the **gas / bubble** point.

5. When checking the subcooling of a Zeotropic refrigerant, the technician must convert the pressure read on the liquid line to the saturated **bubble / dew** temperature.

6. When checking the total superheat of a Zeotropic refrigerant, the technician must convert the pressure read on the vapor line to the saturated **bubble / dew** temperature.

Circle the best answer for each statement/question.

7. Which type of blend refrigerant acts like a single component refrigerant?

    a. Zeotropic   b. Near-Azeotropic

    c. Azeotropic   d. Near-Zeotropic

8. Which type of blend refrigerant is made up of single component refrigerants having very different boiling points?

    a. Zeotropic   b. Near-Azeotropic

    c. Azeotropic   d. Near-Zeotropic

9. Which type of blend refrigerant is made up of single component refrigerants having similar yet different boiling points?

    a. Zeotropic   b. Near-Azeotropic

    c. Azeotropic   d. Near-Zeotropic

10. Which blend refrigerant has the greatest temperature glide?

    a. Zeotropic   b. Near-Azeotropic

    c. Azeotropic   d. Near-Zeotropic

11. A P/T chart that includes bubble and dew must be used with which type of refrigerant blend?

    a. Zeotropic   b. Near-Azeotropic

    c. Azeotropic   d. All of the above

Answer the following with complete sentences.

12. What is fractionation? _____

_____

_____

_____

13. When there is a refrigerant leak in a system with a blend refrigerant, what affects the severity of the mixture change within the refrigerant blend? _____

_____

_____

_____

_____

14. When charging a system with a blend refrigerant, why must the blend refrigerant exit the bottle as a liquid? _____

_____

_____

Complete the following two equations.

15. Blend refrigerant subcooling = _____

16. Blend refrigerant total superheat = _____